Managing & developing People

Managing & developing People

Editor:
Gill Brain

Published by The Staff College
in association with
the Association for Colleges

Published by The Staff College
in association with
the Association for Colleges

Copies of this book can be obtained from:
The Staff College
Coombe Lodge
Blagdon
Bristol BS18 6RG

Commissioning Editor Gillian Brain
Cover design by Susan Leather, The Staff College
Layout and sub-editing by Pippa Toogood, The Staff College
Typesetting by Action Typesetting, Gloucester
Printed in the UK by Booksprint, Bristol, cover films by Triangle, Yatton

ISBN 0-907659-84-5

Contents

About the authors

Gill Anslow. A psychologist by first degree and a personnel manager by training, Gill Anslow began her career in personnel working for Cadbury Schweppes and Imperial Metal Industries. A qualified secondary teacher, Gill spent two years teaching the ROSLA cohort, before moving to a succession of further education jobs at GLOSCAT, Croydon College and Guildford College of Further and Higher Education, where she became Principal in January 1992.

Gill is convinced that quality improvement is pivotal to the enhancement of FE and is key to the achievement of corporate goals and missions. This interest sprang from her involvement with the creation and implementation of the academic quality assurance policy and procedures at Croydon College. Together with Richard Gorringe, she has presented papers at various conferences, both at home and abroad, on the development of total quality management in education. Gill is a current director of the Colleges' Employers' Forum (CEF).

Gill Brain was educated in Jamaica and Southampton before taking a degree in sociology and then a Masters in education research. Entering the work of further education by accident as an assistant lecturer in liberal studies, she then worked in colleges across the country in Hampshire, Bromley, Luton, Yorkshire, London and Birmingham. Her posts have included staff development officer, head of department and vice-principal. Before being appointed to her current job as Principal of Salisbury College in May 1982, she was Principal of Acton College.

Gillian's over-riding interest remains with the students and curriculum, hence an increasing involvement with issues of quality in all its aspects. She borrows good ideas from anywhere and tries to construct a coherent approach to issues of quality in further education.

Richard Chambers began his career as a clerical officer with the Inner London Education Authority for whom he worked for 12 years. He then moved into teaching and spent five and a half years developing and delivering a wide range of management education and training programmes.

Richard's current post is as Assistant Principal at Lewisham College where he holds responsibility for planning and enterprise. This remit includes leading the college's Investors in People project.

Immediately prior to joining Lewisham College, Richard was Senior Assistant Education Officer with Lewisham Education during which time he made cameo appearances in the BBC television series Town Hall.

Richard holds an MSc in education management, the culmination of eight years almost continuous part-time study which started at FE level. As someone who has benefited from the second chance offer made by colleges of further education he is strongly committed to the role they have to play in this area.

Alan Dodson. Prior to incorporation Alan Dodson was Co-ordinator of Staff Development and In-service Training in Hereford and Worcestershire colleges. Originally trained as an analytical chemist, he graduated in 1963 from one of the earliest CNAA courses. He began teaching in 1964, breaking his service to complete a PhD in radiochemistry in 1969. He is a member of The Royal Society of Chemistry and is a chartered chemist.

He has been involved with science teaching, at a local and regional level, as course designer, external moderator, Open University tutor, etc. Like others of his generation he has served a long apprenticeship in the ranks of further education teachers, moving into management later in his career with the aid of his own in-service training via a polytechnic education management diploma.

Alan is a man of varied activities. In particular, he has many friends and interests in France where he is associated with a number of initiatives for students with learning difficulties and special needs.

Currently he is working independently as a lecturer and writer on various aspects of further education and his many other interests.

Helen Gilchrist has been Principal of Nelson and Colne Tertiary College since 1 June 1989. She began her career in education teaching languages in a school. She then moved to Skelmersdale College where she was Vice-Principal. That was followed by a move to North Manchester College – a multi-cultural environment

– as Assistant Principal were she was responsible for all courses within a matrix structure. She then spent three years as Vice-Principal at Accrington and Rossendale College before moving to her present position.

She has a long-standing interest in and commitment to issues concerning women in education and has been the author of a number of reports. She has been a speaker and organiser of a number of staff training conferences and initiatives. She is presently a member of the Association for Colleges.

Richard Gorringe is currently Director of Norton Radstock College, situated outside Bath. He was previously Assistant Director at Crawley College, carrying particular responsibility for quality and human resources. Prior to that, Richard was Assistant Director of Education for the London Borough of Croydon where he was responsible for further and higher education, the adult education service, youth service and careers service.

Richard's previous experience includes 10 years' lecturing in FE in inner London, a period as Senior Staff Development Officer for the County of Avon, and an appointment as one of the first development officers for the National Council for Vocational Qualifications. His chief interests are in quality management and relating the use of resources to curriculum development to create more flexible, accessible colleges. Richard was a member of the Funding Methodology Group set up by the Further Education Funding Council, and now sits on their Tariff Advisory Committee.

Richard has written and contributed to a wide range of publications, topics include achievement-based resourcing and the accreditation of prior learning.

Tony Henry. Tony was educated at the Central Grammar School in Birmingham. He studied at the University of Wales for his degree in English and at the University of Birmingham where he gained his Certificate in Education.

Tony has worked in the field of further education for 21 years and has been Principal of East Birmingham College for the past six years.

John Skitt is currently principal of Barnet College, a post he has held since 1985. His previous experience includes appointments at Luton College of Higher Education, Barnfield College and Middlesex University. He holds a BA and MA from Lancaster University.

A main concern of his has been to support the professional development of staff. John participated in the development of Barnet College's staff development, training and review policies. These schemes have been used as a model in the UK and abroad and have been developed in the context of whole college personnel policy.

John is active in promoting a unified voice for FE and in advocating a strong association if colleges. He is keen to internationalise FE in both curricular terms and in the sharing of practice and experience.

Jan Wagstaff worked as a line and personnel manager in industry for many years before joining the FE sector. She has an MA in management and is a member of the Institute of Personnel Management (IPM). She held management positions in both FE and HE institutions before joining The Staff College as a staff tutor in 1989, where she remained for two years. Previous to that, she spent a year teaching at an American university and researching personnel practices and employment law in the USA.

Now working as a consultant, she has remained an associate tutor of The Staff College and has worked with many college managers and governors in their preparation for incorporation. She is now working with them in planning changes to and introducing innovations in their personnel strategies and practices. She is particularly interested in the relationship between UK and European employment law. Jan has written widely on personnel matters for the education sector and for industry in general.

Preface

Gill Brain

Human resource issues in further education

Further education is an intensely people-centred service and human resource management (HRM), of course, is all about people. The successful management of human resources in our further education colleges is vital to the success of our sector. The study of people in organisations is a fascinating and absorbing one, not only because they are the most complex of organisational variables, but also because they are so vital to organisational success. In the following pages we find a wealth of ideas about and approaches to human resource management in further education colleges. These ideas would be interesting to read at any time but are particularly compelling at the present when the sector is undergoing far-reaching changes. In analysing and developing strategies to handle such change, managers cannot escape from the central importance of human resource management. It pervades all aspects of organisational life and thus all other management functions – financial management, curriculum development, client services, marketing – rely on good human resource management. Since all these other functions are themselves run by teams of people, the relationship with HRM strategies can never be a simple or discrete one. Throughout this book we find many thought-provoking ideas on various aspects of HRM from Investors in People programmes to staff development initiatives; from appraisal to productivity; and from total quality management to pay and performance.

There can be no 'right' way. Each college must find what works for its staff, students and community. However, we hope that in the following chapters you may find some ideas to help you manage your most costly and vital resource. Throughout human history learning has taken place whenever two or more people gather together, often regardless of other variables. It is our task as managers to ensure the most favourable conditions for those gathering together for learning purposes in our organisations. That is the challenge of human resource management.

Chapter 1: Investors in People

Richard Chambers

Introduction

Investors in People is a National Standard, designed to help employers, whether in the public or private sector, to get the most out of their people. Administered by the Employment Department and the training and enterprise councils, achievement of the Standard shows a high degree of commitment by the employer to the training and development of its staff.

This chapter considers how working towards recognition as an Investor in People may support colleges in implementing change and achieving the goals and objectives set out in their strategic plans. It is known that many colleges have already given serious consideration to (or are in the process of) committing to the Investors Standard. The aim of this chapter, therefore, is to describe and comment on Lewisham College's approach to the achievement of the Investors Standard in a way which may assist other institutions in their own evaluations of the potential implications and benefits of working towards such recognition.

There are compelling reasons for colleges to take a strong interest in the Investors in People initiative. The Standard is, of course, concerned with the development of people as a means of improving organisational effectiveness. As people development is the core business of colleges (and no doubt college mission statements will refer to this), it would be odd if the Standard was not widely embraced by the further education sector. Colleges undoubtedly have a major role to play in the achievement of the widely-lauded national education and training targets. Becoming an Investor in People is recognised as being one pathway to achievement of the targets. Furthermore, working towards recognition provides a framework for human resource development which links training objectives to the service plans of colleges. Ability to demonstrate such links will be required by the Further Education Funding Council when stage two of the strategic planning framework is introduced for 1994/95.

The background to Lewisham College's commitment to the Investors Standard

Lewisham is some way through a process of substantial organisational change. A brief chronology of recent key events is set out in **Figure 1**.

Figure 1: Recent key events

pre-April 1990
: Lewisham College was then known as South East London College or 'Seltec'. It fulfilled a role of regional significance under the Inner London Education Authority's strategic planning of further education.

1 April 1990
: the college transferred to Lewisham (and became Lewisham College) and engaged in the difficult task of refocusing its role. The local authority's statutory responsibility was to secure adequate further education provision for Lewisham people and inevitably the emphasis in planning was on local rather than regional need.

1 September 1991
: a new principal (Ruth Silver) took up post.

1 December 1991
: new governing body formed in readiness for financial delegation (this took place later in inner London than in other areas).

1 April 1992
: financial delegation takes place.
Many middle managers take early retirement,

  phased college restructuring is initiated,

  a draft of the college's strategic plan for the period 1993–98 is published.

1 May 1992 onwards
: Plans for incorporation set and put in train, including:

  June 1992 key appointments in the new structure made.

  September 1992 – January 1993 new senior managers take up post.

  1 January 1993 – 31 March 1993 second phase of restructuring undertaken.

1 April 1993
: incorporation.

Looking to the future, the college will be commencing the implementation of its five year plan which includes objectives for substantial growth in student numbers and significant developments in the character and style of service delivery. As far as internal organisation is concerned, the college will work towards the delegation of management responsibilities to its new faculties, allowing them maximum freedoms to develop provision with the overall framework of the strategic plan, supported by strong corporate systems.

Now I have briefly described key points in the past and future agenda for change, it is important to record something about the organisational context in which change has been taking place. Four factors are particularly relevant here.

First, Lewisham College did not have a strong corporate planning culture. This may have been a legacy of the Inner London Education Authority's centralised planning approach but, as a result, the college was not well equipped to anticipate and take charge of the changes it was to face following its transfer to Lewisham.

Second (and a more specific version of the first point), key corporate functions – notably financial and human resource management – were underdeveloped. Institutionally-based activity could be characterised as the local administration of centrally managed policies, systems and procedures. Late delegation in inner London, although inevitable, meant that the task of achieving a state of basic readiness for incorporation within the time available was enormous. It is evident that the functional and role changes arising from delegation and incorporation have been, and will continue to be, testing for learning support staff. These staff, therefore, have had to live with a very high level of uncertainty.

Third, on the academic side, the college is now putting in place a management and organisational structure which will enable it to deliver its mission and strategic plan. However, as the timescale reveals, the college operated without the benefit of an experienced middle manager layer from April to December 1992. This, and a widely held appreciation that academic leadership priorities will be defined by future aspirations of the college rather than past norms and conventions, has meant that the past year has been a stressful period of transition for lecturing staff.

Fourth, the college experienced three years of particularly severe financial cuts, first made under the control of ILEA and then with Lewisham LEA. Viewers of the television series 'Town Hall' will have an appreciation of the financial turbulence which surrounded the college (as well as other education and council-run services) in the 1991/2 financial year. Compulsory redundancies took place and these, combined with uncertainty about the future prospects for the institution, placed a severe strain of the vitality of the college.

In summary then, Lewisham College has had to manage four eras of being within three years (ILEA to Lewisham to delegation to incorporation).

Within this time-frame it has had to manage the effects of deep financial cuts as well as develop its vision for the future. The college has a strong vocational education tradition and is well placed, by virtue of this and the undisputed skills of its teaching force, to meet national policy objectives for the remainder of the decade. Through restructuring, the college is developing a form which will support the achievement of its future objectives. However, it is seeking to move into a future from a recent past characterised by considerable organisational stress and change. Ultimately, the college's future success will depend on the ability of all its staff to adapt to their new roles and to contribute towards the achievement of the college's objectives. It is this context which provides the rationale for the college's commitment to the Investors Standard. In short, becoming an Investor in People will be a significant tool through which the college will become 'fit for the future'.

Lewisham College's route to recognition

The college's formal route to recognition as an Investor in People began with the development of strategic alliances by the principal with key external agencies during the autumn of 1991. The purpose of forming these alliances was to increase external understanding of the college's current position, its future potential, and to identify potential bases for partnerships and mutual support.

Part of the response from the chief executive of the South Thames Training and Enterprise Council was to offer support through the business growth training and Investor in People schemes to facilitate the developments which the college needed to undertake. At this time the Investors in People scheme was only just opening up to public sector organisations. For the training and enterprise council (TEC), the college's involvement offered an early opportunity to explore the issues involved in applying the Standard in the public sector.

Following agreement by the college's finance and general purposes committee, the principalship undertook an initial management survey with the support of an external consultant. Given that the college at this stage had not formulated its strategic plan, and what has been said earlier about the underdevelopment of the human resource management function, it was not surprising that the outcome of the analysis was a confirmation that achievement of the Standard needed to be viewed as a long-term objective. Nevertheless, it was clear that the Standard offered a robust framework for the planning of human resource development and the commitment work towards recognition became an integral part of the college's draft strategic plan for 1993–98, which was endorsed by governors in April 1992.

Achievements to date

It is assumed that most readers will be familiar with the four sections of the Investors in People Standard but it may be helpful to recap these here:

- public commitment from the top to develop all employees to achieve business objectives;

- regular review of training and development needs of all employees in line with business objectives;

- action to train and develop individuals on recruitment and throughout their employment; and

- evaluation of the investment in training and development to assess achievement and improve future effectiveness.

Work since April 1992 has concentrated on the first two sections of the Standard. Specific actions are summarised below as follows:

- the college's vision, mission, strategic objectives and draft plan for the period 1993–98 were first issued April 1992;

- as noted above, integral to the plan is a commitment to work towards the achievement of the Investors in People Standard is integral to the plan;

- the content and achievability of the plan was interrogated by a strategic audit of the college conducted by consultants. The audit identified some specific areas of staff development need during the summer of 1992;

- presentations of the strategic plan have been made to all sections/departments within the college;

- an initial assessment of the staff developed implications of the strategic plan was made during summer 1992;

- the college's operating statement for 1993/94 has related staff development to training objectives.

Work which is now in train includes:

- identification of the development and support needs of those filling new posts within the college's new structure;

- designing and establishing piloting arrangements for the college's development review process – this is the college's appraisal scheme;

- designing the employee survey so that staff can contribute ideas for the future planning and evaluation of staff development and training activity, as well as providing information on current staff perceptions on this subject;

- designing a recruitment induction pack and programme for new staff;

- developing an employees' charter (a pilot version of a students' charter was introduced in September 1992);

- a series of presentations for staff on the Investors in People Standard to improve levels of understanding;

- the development of a standards manual for the institution based on work done by organisational teams.

Commentary

As indicated earlier, the attainment of the Investors Standard will be a three to four year project at Lewisham College. This timescale is dictated in part by the baseline from which it is operating. As described earlier, the college has had to move at some speed to put in place the basic organisational building blocks needed to move successfully towards incorporation and act as a sound basis for future development. While staff have been kept informed and have been consulted on key issues and developments, much of the drive for change in the recent past has of necessity come from the top. The challenge for the future is therefore, to make internal planning processes iterative so that strategic direction and priority both inform and are informed by, activity and decision-making at the operational level. Achieving such planning dialogues will be necessary if staff are to develop a stronger sense of being stakeholders in the future of the organisation. It is through such a process that staff may come to identify their own aspirations for development with those of the college. The task is a substantial one given the range and numbers of staff employed in a college the size of Lewisham. It is made more challenging still given the barriers to communication which are inherent with a multi-site operation and the expected rise in the numbers of part-time workers who may perceive they have (and indeed be perceived to have) a limited contractual relationship with the college.

From this perspective, committing to becoming an Investor in People does not look like an easy option for those colleges not in the happy position of being well placed to achieve readily the award by virtue of established human resource strategies and systems. This, in the author's view, raises a number of questions which colleges need to consider both prior to and after the decision whether to commit.

Working towards recognition as an Investor in People is an act which enters the external public domain (via published lists). For this reason it is less likely to be a decision which organisations will take on the basis that they can quietly shrink back from it at a later date for whatever reasons. Hence a commitment to the Investor Standard is a commitment to invest manager time and energy over an extended period in the formulation of strategies and systems for human resource development. This is a positive thing if one takes the view that (and it seems doubtful that many would publicly disagree) the quality of service offered to learners will be positively influenced by having a workforce whose skills are continuously and systematically developed and upgraded. This said, long-term change processes are vulnerable to problems of momentum. Crowded management agendas and the indistinct path between now and the future both act as forces of inertia. Allied to this, institutions need to consider how to manage staff expectations following the decision to commit. The Standard expects the commitment to be made public and many mangers will be very ready to do this. However, Investors in People is a powerful term and it will almost certainly be interpreted by some staff (with or without detailed knowledge of the Standard) as a commitment to meet their aspirations for training and development, whether or not such activity relates clearly to the immediate objectives of the organisation.

This leads to the need to consider the potential impact of the Investors Standard on staff development practices in institutions. The following issues may need to be considered:

- staff development and training plans need to be driven by service planning. The question of ownership of and stakeholding in service planning has already been discussed;

- the development needs of all staff have to be addressed. This may mean the inclusion of a wider range of staff in staff development activities. It will also almost certainly mean that voluntary or demand-led participation in training will be replaced by a stronger element of requirement.

Training and development activities should lead to a difference in organisational performance – that is, the investment has a measurable pay back. By all accounts and perhaps not surprisingly, this is the area of the Standard which causes organisations the most difficulty. For many colleges this aspect almost certainly calls for further development of in-house training capability and/or exercising far greater selection in the use of externally provided training opportunities.

Judging by views expressed in locally and nationally convened Investors in People workshops, it would appear that the above factors (in a variety of combinations) represent a source of tension, the more so where staff expectations of the training and development opportunities which ought to be available have been defined by reference to historical norms and conventions rather than organisational needs.

This raises a range of issues. First, reluctance to participate in training activities will need to be challenged through managers being prepared to explicitly state the possible implications of staff not upgrading or extending their skills. Hopefully, initial reluctance will give way to a recognition of need but persistence will almost certainly be necessary with some individuals.

Second, colleges will need to consider how the benefits of more broad-based development activities (notably long courses) can be evaluated. It is likely that managers will have to dedicate more time to supporting individuals to apply the learning to practice through mentoring or other mechanisms.

Third, institutions will need to consider how, within the framework of the Standard, they respond to staff who wish to undertake training or development activities to prepare or position themselves for future roles rather than the ones they hold at present. This implies a need for career planning systems which take account of future human resource needs and, where relevant, institutional commitment to improving equality of opportunity for staff. If staff development and training programmes are not informed by a future perspective or they are not interrogated in terms of institutional values, then the under-representation of women and people from ethnic minority backgrounds (for example) at particular points in the organisational structure are not likely be addressed through attempts to reach the Standard.

It is not the task of this chapter to speculate in any detailed way on how staff terms and conditions of service may change or, indeed, have changed, as a result of incorporation. What is clear from public expenditure forecasts for the next three years is that planned growth in the further education sector is to be achieved by a mix of additional investment and improvements in productivity. Regardless of the specific ways colleges seek to further enhance efficiency, the need now to improve productivity is bound to place new demands on college staff. I feel it is important that colleges invest in training and development of staff in a way which enables them to respond to such demands. The Investors in People Standard offers a framework for doing this.

Perhaps more significantly, commitment to the Standard may be an important feature of the new relationships which develop between corporations and their employees over the next few years. Specifically, commitment *and* action to invest in staff will provide tangible evidence that colleges continue to see staff as their most valuable resource. Such confirmation may be important at a time when the framework for the conduct of employee relations is undergoing change.

Summary and conclusions

This chapter has described Lewisham College's rationale for working towards achievement of the Investors in People Standard and progress made to date. It has attempted to illustrate that making a commitment to achieve the Standard will represent a substantial undertaking for colleges which have not formulated strategies and systems for reviewing the training needs of staff within the framework of their institutional plans. Comment has been made on some of the issues which colleges may face in the implementation of their action plans.

It is right and appropriate that individual institutions will approach the achievement of the Standard in a way that fits local circumstances. This said, it is worth considering how benefits to colleges and employees can be maximised. It seems to me that three issues could be particularly significant. First, the degree of ownership of college objectives. This may be increased by staff involvement in planning decisions. If such involvement can be increased through delegation, there is likely to be a greater coincidence between development and training needs identified by managers and staff. Second, working with the Standard may lead to changes in staff development practices. Some of these changes may be difficult to manage because Investors in People initiatives come to be perceived as providing less freedom for staff to choose the activities they wish to engage in and a stronger element of requirement. For this reason, it appears to be particularly important that staff development planning addresses both short-term and longer-term time horizons so that future career planning can be supported. Third, making the commitment to achieve the Investors Standard is timely since it can become part of the new relationship between further education corporations and their workforces.

Achievement of strategic plans will ultimately depend on those who deliver services to learners. In turn, the livelihoods and career prospects of the staff depend on the success of their employers. This mutual dependency has always existed but it has become more explicit since incorporation. Developing people in ways which enable them to respond to expectations and demands may make the process of change easier and the chances of institutional success that little bit more certain.

Chapter 2: Total quality management

Richard Gorringe
and
Gill Anslow

Introduction

The purpose of this chapter is to:

- describe briefly what is meant by total quality;
- describe a method for developing quality standards; and
- suggest some means of devising and monitoring achievement in relation to quality standards.

Quality is one of the key issues facing corporate colleges. Further education has been bombarded by a variety of initiatives including BS 5750, Investors in People and total quality management (TQM). This chapter attempts to place TQM in a college context and balance it with economic imperatives for increased efficiency and effectiveness.

TQM is not a panacea for all the ills facing us but rather stresses a pragmatic approach to handling the quality discussion in a strategic way. All colleges will be required by the Further Education Funding Council (FEFC) to produce their plans for quality control and development as part of the new inspection framework. This chapter presents a cogent way of improving the educational process by focusing on inputs and outcomes within the TQM spirit.

In contrast to other approaches to quality, TQM embraces fully the notion of quality teams at all levels in an institution: associated staff development is a *sine qua non*. The 'customer' (usually the student) assumes his or her rightful place within the planning framework: planning is seen as more than juggling the budget or predicting student enrolment trends. Within a college which has fully embraced TQM, the customer is at the heart of all its activities. TQM methodology underlines the need to perceive customers as external and internal. This recognition can bring about a change in culture within the organisation and thus lead to improvements in quality.

TQM should be seen for its worth – an aid to increasing quality within a learning institution.

Total quality: what is it?

There are many accounts of total quality. One way of approaching it is to say that it is a style of managing what an organisation does which brings people, resources and systems together around the concept of continuous quality improvement. This implies that a major feature of total quality is that it refers to the wishes and needs of customers outside the organisation. This raises several issues when applying the concept to education: there can be ambiguity over who our customers are. Everyone can be seen as both a customer and supplier to someone else throughout the college. Explanations of total quality, however, are probably less important than grasping the essential concept that it involves a particular way of managing an organisation. Anyone who is involved in managing will need to understand and relate to it.

Towards a model for total quality

In a college, a model for total quality could be built from two basic quality improvement precepts. The first precept is that the organisation must be managed to 'do things right'. The second, that it must also ensure that it is 'doing the right thing' (see **Figure 1**). Doing things right refers to ensuring that the inputs to the educational process, the process itself, and the outputs of it, are the best and most suitable to the purpose that can be achieved.

> *inputs* cover the learning environment, staff experience and qualifications, books, materials, equipment available, etc.;
>
> *process* covers the learning modes available, care and concern for the learner, etc.;
>
> *outputs* cover the achievement of learners, satisfaction indices, etc.

Doing the right thing, however, is fundamentally important because, no matter how well a programme is taught, it cannot be fully effective if it is inaccessible to many customers who wish to benefit, or if the skills and knowledge on offer are no longer useful for their intended purpose, e.g. obtaining a job. Total quality is a

Figure 1: Systematic quality improvement: action model

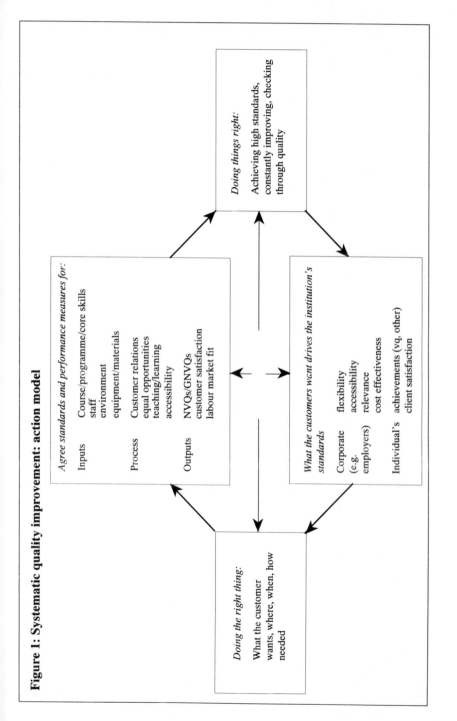

Agree standards and performance measures for:

Inputs	Course/programme/core skills
	staff
	environment
	equipment/materials
Process	Customer relations
	equal opportunities
	teaching/learning
	accessibility
Outputs	NVQs/GNVQs
	customer satisfaction
	labour market fit

Doing things right:

Achieving high standards, constantly improving, checking through quality

What the customers want drives the institution's standards

Corporate (e.g. employers)	flexibility
	accessibility
	relevance
	cost effectiveness
Individual's	achievements (vq, other)
	client satisfaction

Doing the right thing:

What the customer wants, where, when, how needed

23

combination of proactivity in relation to what is wanted (including how, when, where programmes are required) with painstaking management of how things are actually delivered. From this it is clear that wider questions of the college mission, how it relates to external changes, and how it manages its internal processes, are involved. As Ron Collard says:

> Achieving quality standards within organisations is about attitudes at all levels. Quality is not just about systems, it is not just about using specific techniques and tools, or complying with BS 5750.
>
> Quality is about the attitude of mind of all the individuals within organisations, it is about winning the hearts and minds not only of them but also of customers who must come to believe that the organisation produces goods or services which meet their specific requirements. Creating an environment and implementing a programme which recognises the crucial importance of attitudes in an organisation is the key to the long-term success and profitability of that organisation.
> **Total quality: success through people** (Collard 1993)

A college can only embrace total quality if those who are responsible for defining what kind of institution it is; which customers it wishes to serve; and what its purpose or mission is; have set out answers to these questions in a strategy. Senior managers have two main strategic roles in relation to quality:

- gathering intelligence on the future changes in customers, their wishes and needs, and the environment (financial, demographic, organisational) which the college faces; and

- applying this intelligence to strategic thinking about the future and how structures and processes in the college must change to deliver what is required in the best possible way.

One way of expressing both what the college as a whole needs to do, and what its schools or departments need to do individually, is to devise a set of success factors. (See **Figure 2** for critical success factors devised at Guildford College for the college as a whole.) These are simple statements of what is needed at each level to create a successful high quality college, and in relation to which actual achievement can be judged.

The concept of continuous quality improvement in an ever changing environment requires, in addition to a supportive culture and strategy, a set of management tools to control and monitor what is actually going on in the college. Based on the model of both doing the right thing, and doing things right, appropriate standards

Figure 2: Critical success factors – Guildford College of Further and Higher Education

The successful implementation of the corporate plan depends crucially on all of us, but especially the corporate management team getting a number of points right over the next four to five years. These critical success factors can be identified as follows.

Quality

The commitment to quality in the plan requires that we have a clear understanding of what quality means in practice, at all levels of the college's operation. It means, too, that appropriate quality improvement processes have to be established and used to monitor quality and determine action.

Flexibility

Matching needs of potential customers and widening access to the college entails delivery of a genuinely flexible curriculum. This goes beyond modularisation and is much more about responding positively and imaginatively to customer needs. It is also about anticipating and shaping these needs. The goal, explicit in the plan, is not merely to survive but to grow and to thrive.

Marketing

To respond to these needs we have to identify them. To do that we have to get closer to the customer at both the strategic and operational levels. This includes improving the quality, in breadth and in depth, of our market research. It includes improving our links with industry, the schools and the community at large. Critically, it means the development of a market-driven product portfolio delivered in the most cost-effective way.

Financial management

The goal of cost-effectiveness has obvious implications for the way we manage our financial affairs. It goes without saying that we must develop and implement sound financial practices to the highest commercial standard. More than this, however, their purpose needs to be explained and understood. On incorporation the college will come into possession of valuable assets. It is clearly imperative that these assets are managed effectively.

Management information

Sound financial management will be greatly aided by the development of an effective management information system. This will have applications going well beyond the requirements of financial control and will upgrade the quality of decision-making throughout the college.

Staff

The staff of the college is by far its most important asset. Their support for this plan will be the most critical factor of all in its success. For this reason it is essential that we inaugurate personnel management policies and procedures that will release the talents of our staff. This can be achieved by locating decision-making in its most appropriate place, to give staff a genuine voice in making the decisions that affect them. Just as important, it demands a commitment from the corporate management team to communicate, to listen and to inform.

and performance measures for all the college processes can be derived. It is necessary to write these down (e.g. in a series of manuals for example) and to devise systems to monitor the standards in practice, and report back to those in a position to make change when required. It is from these needs that a formal quality management system like BS 5750 or IS 09000 arises. Such a system can only operate when the actual standards have been agreed: the system can help to meet them, it cannot decide what they should be.

A common approach to standard-setting is to focus on each operational unit within the college, e.g. school, department or other service, and ask those who are responsible for delivery to devise appropriate standards. Those closest to the college's customers are in the best position to understand and meet their needs. Such standards would cover doing things right (how potential students will be interviewed, inducted and generally treated for example), what will be asked of them, and what will be provided by staff in return. Senior, and to some extent middle, managers will also be responsible for standards for doing the right thing, e.g. for accessibility, validity and flexibility of programmes. This will involve standards for college learner services, e.g. admissions, accreditation of prior learning (APL), guidance, and for corporate activities such as marketing, modularisation, accreditation.

In a total quality college, quality is being audited all the time by everyone. All staff know the agreed standards for their particular role, e.g. standards for course provision are known and used by all course team members, or standards for the physical condition of the building are known and operated by maintenance staff. In a sense everyone is a quality manager and is both required and empowered to deliver quality.

A quality audit is really a way of asking the questions: 'Are you really doing what you say you are?' and 'Are the standards written down being operated rigorously in practice?' A course, a school, a college service, are all possible areas for audit. The key is that the intended standards and procedures are known and defined. For example questions such as 'Are you a good teacher?' which are undefined and imprecise are phrased 'Is the quality of learning and teaching on offer meeting the standards we have agreed to achieve quality?'

Colleges which are certificated to BS 5750 or IS 09000 receive audit from British Standards Institution (BSI) inspectors, or equivalent, at regular intervals. Otherwise the process usually involves a short-life audit team from some other part of the college. In this way, many staff can experience both the audit and auditor role.

Total quality is not one idea or activity; it is a management methodology which permeates the whole institution, its culture, values and processes. Although training courses can be mounted to explain and plan strategies for total quality, the real training and development takes place everyday as new ways of working are pursued. Nevertheless, there will need to be workshops and other training and development activities on standard setting, devising and implementing a quality management system, undertaking a quality audit, using the management information systems (MIS), and many other things.

Getting started

At Crawley and Guildford colleges, a key condition for total quality has already been met: that of commitment from the principal and top management. The issue now is to devise a programme of action and development that will enable everyone to participate and feel the benefits. It is perhaps as well to set these out straightforwardly at the beginning. **Figure 3** is adapted from Ron Collard.

Figure 3: Benefits of a TQM approach

College		*Staff*
Improved quality		Job satisfaction
Improved use of resources		Participation
Greater efficiency		Training and development
Better relationships		Status/recognition
	Everybody benefits	

Customers

Greater satisfaction
Higher achievement
Trust and continuity

A clear management strategy is necessary. As a minimum such a strategy should state:

– what we want to achieve as a college, e.g. objectives, client groups, market positioning:

– what values we bring, e.g. equality of opportunity, respect for individuals, valuing of people regardless of official positions;

- how we are going to achieve it, e.g. the structures, learner services which will be on offer;

- how we shall know if we are achieving it, e.g. our quality management and reporting systems.

The strategy is the starting point for defining quality because it enables everyone to understand the kind of college they work and learn in, and how it will judge itself, for example through the use of critical success factors. It is important that all staff, including support staff, feel involved in this definitional process which is itself part of culture building. The strategy is then the basis on which departments, course teams and all other services and units define their purposes and set standards for quality.

One common thread in the literature on quality and quality monitoring systems is that the temptation to rush in and impose a system must be resisted. Colleges are extremely complex institutions, with quite different cultures in different vocational areas. At the least, it is time well spent to map the structures and try to understand different points of view. This usually has interesting results in that there will be many examples of good practice, exciting and innovative work, sometimes hidden from the official communication channels in the college. It is important to celebrate these and bring them into common knowledge. An institutional mapping and a cultural audit will provide information for all to share about the institution. Colin Turner (1990) has set out a very interesting approach in **Mendip Paper MP007** on organisational culture.

Beginning from the college strategy, it is necessary to have a mission statement, strategic and operational objectives, standards and measures for all courses, programmes and other college services. This would be a daunting task for one person or group in the college, even if it were appropriate. This is where the institutional mapping comes in. Each department, section, service, is responsible for setting quality standards and agreeing them with senior management. **Figure 4** provides an example.

The lesson here is that people who have devised standards are usually assiduous in implementing them. Involving people in the heart of the quality work is a key feature of total quality. Training can be provided on how to set standards but the key is that the wishes and needs of the customer must always be paramount.

Figure 4: example of part of quality system

Customer services unit

1. *Mission*
   To enable both individual and corporate customers to receive the college services they need in optimum time.

2. *Strategic objectives*
   For example, telephone enquiries are answered promptly and the customer is directed to the correct source of information.

3. *Operational objectives*
   For example, establish one college telephone number and one enquiry point permanently staffed in all schools/units.

4. *Standards*
   For example   Telephone answered within three rings.
   Greeting: 'Guildford College, how can I help you?'
   Enquiry received and passed to correct point first time.

5. *Measures/targets*
   For example   95 per cent of calls answered in three rings.
   Standard greeting used in 100 per cent of cases.
   All enquiries logged.
   98 per cent of calls dealt with in one transfer.

Eventually, the standards described above will become the heart of the quality management system, but a simple linear development is not possible because the process needs to be revisited many times on the road to total quality. A college needs quality management while the process unfolds. At minimum, we need two processes:

- an academic quality assurance process by which new courses and programmes are examined by, for example a programme validation and review committee, to ensure that standards for input, process and output are at acceptable levels; and

- a reporting process by which a basic picture of enrolments, costs and achievements is built up at course, school, and whole college levels.

These will need to feed into existing college management information systems, which may have to be modified. Their exact nature will depend on the present arrangements, and will be built from them.

Developing quality standards

This section provides practical guidance on how to develop quality standards for all operations within the college, both within course teams/departments, and in support services. They are based on the methods developed by Sonia Inniss and John Miller (see especially **Managing quality improvement in further education: a guide for middle managers,** 1990).

Before quality can be measured or judged it is necessary to define it. Broadly, the total quality approach suggests that each operational unit in the college may see itself as both a *customer* and *supplier* to others. In defining quality it is necessary to define the product or service which is being supplied, and then define the standards that are required by the customer. The customer may be external, e.g. a potential student, or internal, i.e. other members of staff.

For college courses and programmes there are three aspects of quality to consider:

- the *excellence* of the course/programme itself, i.e. the extent to which the learning opportunities and associated services contribute to customer achievement and satisfaction;

- the *validity* of the course/programme, i.e. the extent to which it meets actual customer needs; for example, a course designed to lead to employment in electrical engineering can only do so if it has the right content and associated qualification, however excellent it is in itself;

- the *accessibility* of the course/programme, i.e. the extent to which intended customers can gain access; for example, is delivery flexible enough? Are there any barriers to access for particular groups?

All the above need to be considered in relation to the college strategy. The *strategy* directs the focus for quality standards by setting out what the college wishes to achieve for its customers; for example, the strategy sets out objectives and targets for the provision of customer information and guidance, flexible modes of delivery, etc. It follows that course/programme teams will need to ensure these are available, and set out quality standards for them. A simple model of quality is:

college strategy + customers' needs and wishes = quality.

It is first necessary to define the function which each course/programme team and other support service in the college performs. For example, for a course team, the function could be provision of learning opportunities and associated services to students wishing to gain a qualification in construction. For the marketing service, it could be provision of market information and development of markets for all college products and services.

The next step is to decide the appropriate quality characteristics for achieving the function concerned. These are those aspects of the service which represent quality. For example, Inniss and Miller (1990) divide provision of a course into four stages, each of which has quality characteristics:

Stage	Quality characteristics (example)
Before entry	unbiased guidance and counselling;
At entry	assistance with study skills;
During course	varied and appropriate learning strategies;
At exit	high levels of achievement.

This method will work well for all other college operational units and services.

The next step is to develop *quality standards* for each quality characteristic. These simply state the standard, setting a target where appropriate, which will be pursued. using the course/programme example:

Quality characteristics	Quality standard
Unbiased guidance and counselling	All applicants will be offered a 15 minute interview with a non-partisan member of staff.
Assistance with study skills	All students will have access to a structured programme covering: – note taking, – revision, – planning and sequencing work.
Varied and appropriate strategies	Programmes to include lectures, seminars resource-based learning, so that no single day is spent in one learning mode.
High levels of achievement	At least 95 per cent success rate in terms of course/qualification objective.

It is important to set standards which are measurable, and which contain a numerical target, e.g. achievement rate, or reference to 'all students'.

The next step is to state *how* the standards will be monitored so that information can be fed back and acted upon. This could be done by developing appropriate performance indicators, which may be informal (e.g. a check sheet of some kind) or formal (e.g. calculation of a *rate* for achievement, progression, etc.).

Conclusion

This chapter has attempted to indicate the benefits of using a total quality management framework within colleges. In particular, whilst stressing the benefits such an approach will bring, it has carefully stressed that TQM is not a panacea to curing quality ills.

Used systematically, within a supportive management culture, TQM recognises the central purpose of quality within institutions whose missions are to provide quality learning, whilst being learning institutions themselves.

References

Collard, Ron (1993) **Total quality: success through people.** Institute of Personnel Management

Inniss, Sonia and John Miller (1990) **Managing quality improvement in further education: a guide for middle managers.** Consultants at Work

Turner, Colin (1990) Organisational culture. **Mendip Paper MP007** Blagdon, The Staff College

Chapter 3: Embedding a professional development culture

Alan Dodson

Background and introduction

In further education we have become so accustomed to constant change there is the danger that we are hardened to it, so that its real effect is diminished. It is certainly true that in the midst of the present welter of activity for change it is not always easy to detect where value is being added to the service and where it is being lost. Indeed, any consideration at the present time is an experience rather like walking on the beach. The pebbles at one's feet alter constantly and yet the general surroundings have much the same design. It is easy to lose track of how far one has come unless you stop from time to time and look back. Unless you have a marker such as the water's edge to follow, how easy it is to go round in circles.

Making proposals for the future of staff development in the colleges conjures up the same images. New ideas are revealed as not-so-new if we stop and look back. Professional development itself for college staff is certainly not a new initiative and has been the subject of countless reports, advisory circulars and occasional action from central and local government for years. As long ago as 1971 staff tutors at the Further Education Staff College were already making that same point and in collected papers they included details of staff development policies and programmes firmly established in a number of colleges (Simmons *et al.* 1971).

What has changed of course is that the 'technology' of staff development has improved. College management itself has improved, opportunities for training have widened, and above all the attitudes and appreciation of the rank and file staff have altered. Staff development has moved forward from those pioneering days in the same way as any science moves forward by the evolution of ever better models to replace those already in existence.

Prominent among these evolutionary stages have been the government grants available under the various related LEA training grant schemes referred to as

Grant-Related In-Service Training (GRIST), LEA Training Grants Scheme (LEATGS), and Grants for Education Support and Training (GEST) from 1987 to 1992. A detailed analysis is not necessary for this review, however some mention is essential. For those colleges whose experience of providing or managing staff development was limited in 1987, the structure of the schemes has had a profound influence at a time when colleges were being moulded by an unprecedented number of other developments including the two major Acts of Parliament. Whilst the constraints of the schemes have not permitted comprehensive professional development in its widest sense to take place, they have shaped and continue to shape colleges' ideas of in-service training.

The resulting volume of training undertaken as a consequence has enabled colleges in broad measure to keep pace with the innovations in curriculum, management and relationships with new and established clients. For LEAs the schemes have been a vehicle for influence and advice. By 1992 the broad aim of LEA in-service training initiatives was to assist colleges in the formation of systems and structures needed for survival in the current climate. The belief expressed in this review is that existing staff development practices must quickly evolve even further so that a full professional development culture exists in all colleges. Such a culture already partially exists but is not yet a feature of college life in general. It is an essential part of staff support if the institutional development which is becoming more readily visible is to continue and to thrive.

Many times in the past I have used the word 'coherent' when describing worthwhile staff development plans and programmes. However, it has not always been understood. In (not quite facetious) response I have said that if the plan is not coherent then it is probably incoherent. This is much better understood. Alternatively, I fall back on scientific analogies and say that when the plan is coherent then it is 'all on the same wavelength' like a laser.

I suspect that the word 'culture' as applied to institutions might give rise to similar difficulties, and in defence I turn to readily available definitions. For example, Wright (1988) quotes several, mostly from management training authors of the mid-1980s. These definitions all have in common the idea of sharing attitudes, beliefs and values throughout the institution. This is the measure of coherence which is not widespread in colleges at present, and which professional development can provide and support.

At the heart of the matter the concept of a professional development culture for staff touches many aspects of college management. Where the culture is changing or needs to change, management development must be at the very leading edge of activity.

To take a simplified example, if one assumes that current external influences and consequent activities in colleges are related as in **Figure 1**, it can be seen that 'management' as a process is at the very core. However, so also is the concept of the whole body of the teaching and other staff as an available resource. This is because the review processes identified below the line can only properly be served by management information which is the outcome of a comprehensive professional development programme.

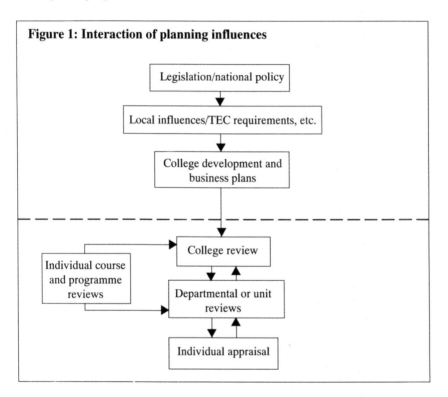

Figure 1: Interaction of planning influences

Legislation/national policy

Local influences/TEC requirements, etc.

College development and business plans

College review

Individual course and programme reviews

Departmental or unit reviews

Individual appraisal

The INSET legacy

As grant-aided training schemes have developed, along with the sophistication of those managing them (usually at LEA-level), several issues have emerged that are important to any successful staff development activity.

The necessity now, even more so than in the past, is the identification and analysis of training needs – always theoretically part of the process, although there are few illusions about how well it has generally been done, even in the early days of LEATGS.

Training should be directed to specific groups of staff

This appears at first to contradict the notion of entitlement, but it need not. The issue is not to suggest that any staff be precluded from training, but rather to underscore the relationship between training and institutional planning.

Entitlement and eligibility

Staff should be entitled to training as a support to help them do their job well. Such a recommendation implies the use of a staff skills audit as a part of existing procedures: this is a theme which is repeated throughout this chapter.

Participation by the staff in training programmes has to be seen as an entitlement. In the wider world of training this idea is not at all new. Indeed, it has been promoted by far sighted managers for years, but is far from being a widespread practical reality.

For colleges, eligibility rather than entitlement is a concept which is easier to accept, because in the harsh world of constrained budgets it can be tempered by complementary notions of priority.

College managers have rapidly gained the skills and experience of training management, but it has frequently been the grant-aid schemes themselves which have dominated their planning. The nearest some college managers have come to the concept of entitlement to training has been their handling of the miscellaneous element in training programmes in response to the diversity of lecturers' work.

Notwithstanding any imperfections in existing staff training and INSET programmes in colleges, these programmes are almost certainly being used as the starting point for developing a system for staff appraisal in most colleges. This approach has been encouraged by the National Joint Council guidelines, which have looked for the best of several worlds in the idea of performance appraisal as a quality indicator but with staff development as the most likely outcome.

This reinforces the idea of an entitlement to training and, if training is an entitlement for staff, then from the college's standpoint it has to be seen as essential underpinning for the development plan. Not all colleges yet have regarded staff development in quite this way. Indeed, some who would argue that they have done so are in reality doing little more than planning INSET alongside their institution development plan rather than as an embedded part of it. Inevitably some colleges are further ahead than others in this aim, but a large number have a surprising distance to go.

Training should be in-house wherever possible

Again the purpose of such a recommendation is not specifically to minimise costs, which it undoubtedly does, but to assist in matching the training to individual college circumstances.

If such individuality was unnecessary then there would be greater efficiency in running training centrally. Such apparent efficiency, however, is a snare for the unwary compared to the effectiveness imbued by college ownership of the training and the resulting motivation towards improved achievement.

Training should be accredited wherever possible

Confusion and hesitancy brought on paradoxically by the very speed of other national developments has made this easier said than done, but some colleges have taken the initiative, usually in partnership with neighbouring HE institutions, and accreditation and credit transfer are beginning to make their mark.

Commitment

Staff should have a commitment to training (that is they should know that training is a part of their job). In the past this has been neither an essential feature of college management nor indeed a necessary progression stage in a lecturer's career. Until recently few lecturers have, for instance, had a detailed job specification or structured progression possibilities around which such a commitment might be framed. Yet these developments have to come, even if in the first instance they are only a knock-on effect of related change.

The legacy of other external influences

Training should, according to the National Council for Vocational Qualifications (NCVQ) philosophy, be competence-based, and should be to national standards. In parallel, but as an independently managed strategy, training should have regard to the requirements of the funding councils and the training and enterprise councils.

In practice this influence is being exerted in several ways, quite apart from any recommendations associated with funding. Some NVQ lead bodies, for example, have adopted virtual closed-shop attitudes in demanding that their assessors and verifiers become qualified to the lead body's occupationally-specific requirements. Effectively this is dictating a component part of college training programmes and was particularly noticeable prior to incorporation.

Foremost during 1992 was the emergence of the Training and Development Lead Body which has published its own standards of competence for qualified trainers, although courses of preparation available at first related only to areas of 'assessment' similar to those of the other lead bodies. By the summer of 1992 all the major awarding bodies in vocational education were in the market place with their versions of so-called generic assessor training.

It is not at all clear whether, in due course, college lecturers as 'full-time trainers' (a term used in the TDLB philosophy) will be expected to show that they conform to the full specification.

Finally, some of the work of lecturers aligns well with the national standards of the Management Charter Initiative (MCI), and probably with the new Guidance and Counselling Lead Body as well, now that government is emphasising this aspect of vocational training in schools as well as colleges and employment training programmes. The Further Education Unit was early on the scene in trying to pilot accredited staff development courses based upon these sets of standards, although it is impossible for any organisation to remain at the leading edge ahead of such rapid change for very long.

Staff development and the pursuit of quality

The thread which links all of these ideas together is the assurance of quality in the staff support systems that colleges might expect to put in to place now that they are incorporated institutions.

The underpinning strategy which relates these issues to each other and to appraisal, is that of undertaking frequent reviews at all levels. One process in particular, consistent with many of the strands of these activities, is the principle of review through self-evaluation. This in its turn may be a component of so-called 'action research'.

Whatever titles are used for these activities (and they are wont to change from time to time), the concept of evaluation as a research technique is particularly useful as a means of ensuring that it becomes regarded as a means to an end and not an end in itself. In this way further planning inevitably emerges, provoking appropriate action.

College lecturers are gradually adapting to the idea of themselves as managers of the learning process, a situation in which self management takes an important role. Few lecturers, however, will be content to adopt the simplest approach to self management, that is building unaided into their work the cyclic programmes of needs identification, action planning, implementation, evaluation, etc. Most will wish to improve their self management by taking advice and thereby calling upon the skills of others in the institution. The relationship to appraisal is immediately apparent.

Similar relationships can be recognised if one accepts the idea that self-evaluation cannot take place in isolation from other processes which are preparative to professional development. A major part of lecturers' duties involve (so-called) classroom teaching. No initiative to embed professional development can ignore the need to make judgements about the quality of what takes place in these situations. One is therefore steered directly to the conclusion that 'classroom observation', or at least the observation of appropriate tasks whose performance can be assessed only in the classroom, has to be a part of the professional development scene. Such observation is not widespread at present except in the context of formal initial training in which it has a different purpose.

Self-evaluation, like all research, requires careful tactics. One such tactic is the compilation of a portfolio of data and other materials, as evidence of achievement in the various components of a job specification. The models for course review developed by a number of LEAs before incorporation include this feature, and might easily be adapted to the personal situation (Avon County Council 1989).

In a sense this closes the loop on the related issues because, not only does compiling a portfolio become a sound technique for use in preparing for appraisal, but it is also a strategy used in context of prior learning assessment and accreditation, and in the use of TDLB and MCI standards, and is therefore at the heart of current professional development thinking.

The promotion of self-evaluation through an analysis of collected evidence, is a doorway through which entry into a professional development culture can be easily and profitably made. It can be particularly valuable in those colleges which have yet to get the basic processes underway.

The implementation of an appraisal scheme requires, or at least provides the opportunity for, the co-ordination of the personnel-related activities which support the quality assurance element of development plans. Hitherto in many colleges these have been relatively unco-ordinated if only because personnel matters have not in the past been managed at local level.

This co-ordination requires the creation of structures appropriate to each college's house style, but which may not yet be present in many colleges. In most cases it also requires an improvement in compatibility and timing of the various review and planning cycles which are in operation. Out of phase planning activities are another legacy of the past likely to cause problems in the future.

Embedding professional development: strategies for implementation

Four practical factors therefore emerge when putting a professional development culture into place in FE colleges:

- college policy;
- management structures;
- co-ordination of the review cycles and appraisal;
- structure and content of the in-house training programme.

Policy

Some colleges still do not have a real policy on staff development. Most, however, do have a set of carefully worded policy statements which represent the senior management's belief of how in-service training should be represented in college. Experience suggests, however, that these statements are written for the benefit of external audiences rather than the staff. Once again the influence of the administrative requirements of the training grant schemes can be felt.

Changing circumstances focus attention on the question of policy in college. This is not to say that a new college policy is essential after incorporation, just that new situations do commonly require that policies are examined, particularly at the tier of decision-making where they (the policies) are turned into practice. A change in external influences is a common cause for policies becoming out of date.

It must be accepted that staff development policies are important. For management they define the decision-making process when training situations arise; for management and others they may define the authority which has been given to put this aspect of staff support into operation.

No policy can be perfect or everlasting and it is almost certain that the time is ripe for each college to look at theirs again, especially if there is any undercurrent of conflict among middle management as to what the training priorities should now be. Since they are the level of management nearest to the curriculum delivery, their views are important, assuming that they have been adequately advised on development matters overall. Unfortunately, this is an assumption which cannot always be made and therefore yet another cause for concern. In the main they will be familiar with the pattern of recent training, but even well presented and 'successful' training activities are no substitute for a sound policy, although often mistaken for it.

Management of the professional development function

Even those colleges which have undergone restructuring, as many have recently, do not all have the coherent structures in place for managing the various aspects of the personnel function in the institution, professional development among them. This relates in the main to the uncertainty of the available budget in the present climate rather than to lack of inclination. The broad need is easily recognised even in those institutions which have so far made little progress. Industrial models of management structures for staff training and development are of course well established. At first glance they seem barely appropriate when transferred to colleges. Nonetheless, a comparison is useful.

In many industrial and commercial companies training and development is a line management responsibility. That is, in a 'good' company, managers and supervisors (perhaps to foreman level) have a practical responsibility for training their subordinates or for getting them trained. There will then be a training manager, at senior level but probably not at the top of the hierarchy, with a responsibility for developing training in response to, or anticipation of, changing circumstances. These responsibilities will include facilitating and providing training internally where appropriate, and advising upon both training activities and policy as required.

An analogy, but also some important differences, can be readily seen among the many recent changes in further education colleges.

First, the management and co-ordination of staff development is only modestly resourced in most colleges, notwithstanding the volume of training and the amount of monitoring which takes place. A few colleges have established staff development teams, especially where they feel able to offer professional development services externally. Most, however, have only some sort of 'staff development officer', inaffordable as a full-time post, and therefore a part of a wider job specification. It is a task not always compatible with the remaining responsibilities of the person concerned, which often do not allow for the measure of specialisation implied in the 'training manager' job described above.

The comparison when it comes to the question of responsibility for managing the training of individuals is less clear. Immediate supervisors do not exist in colleges in the same way as in industry. Where team leaders or senior lecturers for instance are viewed in this light, they are not always recognisable or appropriate as trainer-managers to their mainscale colleagues. However, the concept of mentors is now firmly established in progressive further education thinking. In the planning and direction of training they could easily take the place of the line manager-trainer found in industry. Review and evaluation of the mentor role may then become the feedstock for the 'planner-manager' role for training and development at the level of head of department or similar. There is a danger, of course, of perpetuating a hierarchical approach if this extra tier is introduced, in circumstances where all else points to maintaining as flat a management structure as possible. But with care a nested structure of management staff support begins to evolve providing the medium on which the professional development culture can thrive.

In-house training programmes

In-house programmes are established and developing in the bigger colleges often as a result of budget squeezes, but also in reaction to particular needs which have become through undertaking other activities – college restructuring, or delivering of NVQs for example.

Probably the longest established in-house activity, in the present phase of training, is the use of information technology (IT), an area which is already well supported by accessible external accreditation. Information technology also lends itself readily to open access workshop strategies which can serve as a model for other parts of the training programme.

To date, however, in-house training as well as much externally provided training has been more or less reactive to changing circumstances. That is, programmes of 'deficiency training' have been dominant. The reactions are getting better of course, with growing awareness of 'what might be wanted next year', but this is not the same and is not as effective as a fundamental cycle of repeated opportunities available to staff in support of their professional development.

The keystone of this present proposal is that such a proactive programme is essential. 'What might be needed next year' should not be discarded and can always be regarded as complementary to the core activities. There is, however, no hope of planning complementary activities unless the foundation activities are in place and reliably accessible.

This was the root problem throughout the LEA Training Grants Schemes when developing devolved schemes of INSET management which many LEAs tried to do in line with delegated finance following the 1988 Education Reform Act. In such strategies the LEA and college programmes had to be, and to be seen, as complementary to one another.

In some authorities a strong central programme was constructed at the core with college programmes as appendages. Others found it more valuable, if more difficult, to work the other way round, in order to emphasise the learning value of delegation. In such cases, it has been the LEA programme which has tried to complement the basic college plans – not always easy to do in multi-college authorities, when college developments are growing at different rates. The consequence of this dichotomy has been an almost continuously variable approach to the creation of in-house programmes of activities in colleges. Nevertheless, basic guidelines can be established for the structure of in-house programmes in college. For example, programmes should be:

- based on the individual requirements of the college and its staff. This is not to say that the wheel must be reinvented repeatedly in every college. There are several model programmes already in progress which can be drawn upon and modified to suit;

- modular and repeatedly accessible in a pick-and-mix fashion;

- comprised of various types of development activity, that is not simply or predominantly training 'courses';

- assessed so as to allow credit accumulation. Accreditation models are available. A common and clearly useful one is to aggregate units of activity by time to make up the equivalent of a 'traditional' one or two year certificated course. A number of HE institutions have created certificates of professional studies, diplomas, or MEd programmes in this way;

- divided between training in generic issues and specialist training;

- divided between college directed training and career enhancement;

- divided between initial training modules and further training;

- compatible with or capable of actually including other modules such as those designed to TDLB, MCI standards or by the different examination boards.

The following examples are modules which have appeared in the schemes of various institutions. They will not all have the same delivery strategies, and some will need external contributors, but in the main they are of such a nature as to make them fundamental to a cyclic in-house programme:

- managing one's own professional development;
- managing performance review in courses;
- developing, delivering, and assessing competence-based curriculum;
- developing and managing open learning;
- tutorship, student guidance and counselling;
- managing information technology;
- marketing education;
- tutoring through equal opportunities;
- providing for special educational needs.

Co-ordination of in-house staff development, appraisal, and college planning

In many colleges these co-ordinating structures, as outlined in the sections above, do not adequately exist at present and will need to be created appropriate to the college's house style. In most cases this will also mean altering the timing of the various cycles of planning which occur already or which are now required so that they coincide. On past occasions this proved to be a problem in managing staff development under the LEA Training Grant Schemes where the planning, implementation and budget cycles of adjacent years overlapped, and in any case were all out of phase with the academic year which remains the preferred timing of most colleges' INSET programmes in spite of all else.

Many colleges have never really come to terms with the practice of accommodating within one financial year the management of the INSET associated with two or more academic years. With the budget constraints described above outline planning for the coming year, much less programming the coming year, has often been an exercise completed to satisfy LEA demands rather than for any genuine purpose in college.

Colleges have always had to reconcile the financial and academic years for budget purposes. In government grant schemes they have been denied the ability to carry budgets forward, and in staff development have also been denied any constancy of supported priorities from one year to the next. This frustration at least disappears with the autonomy gained by incorporation. But in anticipation, as grant aid diminished anyway, supplementary funds from college budgets were already in use before any guidance was available from the Funding Council. Even before the end of 1992 it became wise to consider the GEST funding as no more than a supplement to college funds for INSET rather than perhaps the other way round as had been the case previously.

In these new circumstances, the expert consolidation into the college development plan not only of professional development, but also the data collection which both serves and arises from it, is the real core of the extended co-ordination which is needed. With staff development now allied to appraisal interviews, this situation is exacerbated by the commonly proposed two year appraisal interview cycle, and the inevitable spread of individual interviews throughout this time. The resulting challenge for staff who are managing the human resources of the college will be to achieve this co-ordination while different parts of the cycle are running at quite different frequencies as suggested in **Figure 2** (overleaf). Provided adequate critical pathways are mapped sufficiently well in advance, the task is manageable. But commitment is essential and time, as they say in other disciplines, is of the essence.

References

Avon County Council (1989) **Ensuring quality: course review profile.** Avon County Council

Simmons, D D (Ed.) *et al.* (1971) **College management: readings and cases.** Blagdon, the Further Education Staff College [o/p]

Wright, P (1988) The cultural context *in* R Bennett (ed) **Improving trainer effectiveness**, Chapter 10. Gower Publishing Company

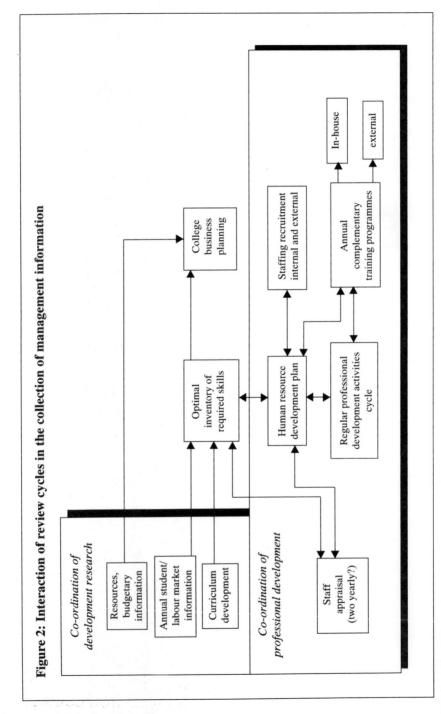

Figure 2: Interaction of review cycles in the collection of management information

Co-ordination of development research

Resources, budgetary information

Annual student/labour market information

Curriculum development

College business planning

Optimal inventory of required skills

Human resource development plan

Staffing recruitment internal and external

Regular professional development activities cycle

Annual complementary training programmes

In-house

external

Co-ordination of professional development

Staff appraisal (two yearly?)

Chapter 4: Changing the culture of human resource development in colleges

Richard Gorringe

Introduction

This chapter describes the ways in which all aspects of managing and developing human resources in colleges are undergoing rapid change. It considers:

- the external environment and reasons for change;
- new approaches being taken by colleges;
- the opportunities and tensions arising; and
- possible future developments.

Some of this material draws on my experience as Assistant Director (Quality and Human Resources) at Crawley College. I should like to thank my colleagues at Crawley, who are too numerous to acknowledge directly, for their contributions to the points made.

Background

Given that colleges were part of the local authority infrastructure, it is hardly surprising that they have historically operated on a public sector model for the recruitment and employment of staff. While often displaying high standards for such matters as ensuring most posts are advertised and therefore widely accessible, the model has firm limitations. These stem from two key sources:

- limitations on the powers of colleges in employment matters; and

- a culture of relatively poorly-rewarded public service which has generally precluded variations between employers such as individual remuneration incentives and non-pay benefits.

Until the Education Reform Act (1988), the local education authority (LEA) was very firmly the employer for all college staff. Governors' powers were circumscribed by a final reference point for employment matters to the authority's education committee. Although recruitment and selection were undertaken by the principal, the influence of the LEA Inspectorate could be strong. In personnel terms, the main work of issuing contracts, conducting probationary years, etc., was carried out by the LEA in all but the largest colleges. In the absence of a dedicated personnel service within colleges it was difficult for a specific 'educational' personnel culture to develop. Indeed, even staff training and development, which most colleges saw as a key responsibility, was treated as a spin-off from the professional work of the college, not as a feature of human resource management.

With the introduction of local management of colleges (LMC), the governing body acquired a number of powers which made them effectively the employer in particular circumstances, although this function remained technically with the local authority. A personnel culture began to grow, focused on the new powers, particularly in the areas of recruitment, retirement, redundancy and parts of employment protection, and race and sex discrimination legislation. Through lack of experience, and the force of the LEA culture, these functions were often carried out as a sort of extension of the Town or County Hall procedures. The LEA personnel manual, containing detailed guidance on pay-scales, grievance, discipline, selection, sickness, maternity, and a host of other matters, was a key reference work.

The underpinning reason for this was the LEA's responsibility for pay determination at national level, and for conditions of service both nationally and locally. The 'Silver Book' containing the national conditions for lecturers, and its sisters the 'Purple Book' (for APT&C staff) and 'White Book' (for manual staff), have had an almost biblical presence. Even now, NATFHE negotiators at national level continue to insist that the Silver Book, albeit with some modifications, is a useful basis for employees' contractural responsibilities.

In personnel terms the Silver Book used to hold a key place as an almost inviolable manual as far as many lecturers are concerned. Although it had no statutory force, it represents the outcome of detailed bargaining to which both sides generally felt commitment. It contained all the strengths and weaknesses of the local government culture of industrial relations. On the one hand it represented what both sides might recognise as some form of compromise between different positions. On the other, as with any nationally agreed conditions of service, it represented rigidities which have been slow to adapt to new realities. The chief problem may be summarised as rigidities in the allocation of the working week and working year between formal scheduled teaching and other duties. This chapter makes the assumption that the move away from these, provided it is done in a context of a commitment to the growth and development of individuals, can be beneficial to staff and college alike.

Beyond this, the dominance of national agreements, and until recently, the legal role of LEAs as employers, have largely prevented the emergence of a mature personnel culture in colleges. Such a new culture requires flexibility – of employment conditions, pay and benefits, and attitudes generally – if it is to flourish. Modern management theory emphasises the key role of people in the success of an enterprise, yet in colleges managing and developing people has been severely constrained by a lack of flexibility.

External pressures for change

Undoubtedly the requirement since 1 April 1993, that colleges operate as independent corporations with responsibility and accountability for financial probity, is the key catalyst for change. However, pressures for change were already present in colleges before this. These pressures stemmed from the fact that lecturers' Silver Book conditions of service have implicit within them a 'model' or set of assumptions about how colleges work. These include:

- a separation between lecturers and all other staff leading, possibly unintentionally, to higher status for the former;

- the primacy of class contact, i.e. a lecturer standing in front of a classroom group as the key pedagogic role;

- the notion that teaching is the key function of a lecturer, rather than the management of learning in a wider sense;

- the view that lecturers are 'academics' who require bursts of teaching activity followed by lengthy periods of recuperation if they are to be effective; and

- the view that traditional patterns of college terms and holidays are the only right way to deliver education and training.

Behind all this, of course, is a narrow view of further education as primarily delivering courses which last from September to June and consist of full-time attendance, day release, block release, etc. When the history of 20th century further education comes to be written it seems inevitable that the national conditions of service will be seen as having a key place in maintaining this model of the educational process long after change was desperately needed.

Since the 1970s, one of the key issues for colleges has been responsiveness to the customer. In essence this means delivering courses and programmes of a wide variety, when, where and how the customer requires. Customers are both individual participants and employers purchasing training. Many colleges have made enormous strides in more flexible hours of attendance, in early morning and weekend classes, bespoke courses, working on employers' premises, drop-in workshops, modular provision, etc.

All this cannot be accommodated within conditions of service designed for another era. Indeed, some colleges adopted the expedient of creating a separate college company, employing staff on new conditions, to make progress.

The key issue here is not that staff should necessarily be working harder, but that ways of working need to be radically different. This is illustrated by the contract introduced in 1991 in the HE sector. This simply specifies an annual working period, and makes the assumption that in a professional culture, the precise mix of duties and working hours will be agreed between lecturers and managers. There may need to be peaks and troughs, but these occur in all the professions. Adopting weekly hourly quotas prevents the emergence of a professional culture of dedicated service and commensurate reward.

Clearly, costs cannot be ignored in any discussion of pressures for change. Once again, the issue should not be seen as one of reducing costs at the expense of staff. It is rather that rigidities actually reduce sensible efficiency, pushing up costs and reducing employment opportunities. Colleges' desire for efficiency is also strongly underpinned by government policy and this is likely to continue for the foreseeable future. The Government has made it clear that the unit of resource per student will fall and has required an efficiency gain of at least three per cent per annum from the Further Education Funding Council (FEFC).

The link between improved efficiency and staffing is a strong one since staff costs may represent 70 to 80 per cent of a college's budget. As in any organisation, staff will perform a variety of roles, for different contracted times, and with varying degrees of application and excellence. The keys to efficient uses of human resources are flexibility in deployment and flexibility in remuneration. There have been effectively only three pay scales which could be used: the lecturers' scale, Administrative, Professional, Technical and Clerical (APT&C) scale, or the manual scale. All are based on the assumption that, by and large, all staff fall neatly into one category, and that the same conditions of service are appropriate for all within the category.

This assumption can cause problems as the following indicates. I recently came across a student outreach worker whose job was to work in the local community to encourage more adults to come to the college, particularly for return to study courses. She was paid as a lecturer, worked 30 hours per week, and was absent throughout the college holidays. Outreach of this kind is required all year round, all day, every day, if it is to stand a chance of being successful. The role could simply not be done by one person in 30 hours per week and with long periods of inactivity during college holidays.

Similarly, there was no requirement for preparation and marking, and no obvious reason why a long incremental pay scale was the best way to reward increasing skill and achievement. This is a classic case of misapplication of a scale. It also demonstrates what can happen when national scales are expected to be used. A culture of examining the real requirements of any post and setting conditions and pay accordingly, just does not develop.

In essence, then, colleges have to become more business-like, if not more like businesses. Efficiency and high performance matter not only because anything less is short-changing both students and tax-payers, but because the organisation itself will not survive without them. This is at the heart of the new further education culture, and therefore, of the corresponding new human resource culture. Quality in all its aspects must be improved. Staff must be rewarded not simply for their subject expertise, but for their excellence in securing achievements for students. Students, and all customers of the service, must be the focal point for understanding and meeting needs. The old impression that the times of opening and general operation of the college were largely designed for the convenience of the organisation must give way to one of a flexible, user-friendly operation.

Some basic issues

The over-riding current issue is to enable staff to feel part of a vibrant, confident organisation which has a mission and purpose, believes in itself, and above all will reward excellence. Human resource planning and treatment of staff need to avoid the impression that distant procedures are being operated which have little connection with individual effort. Every member of staff must feel he or she has a very personal contract, and a personal commitment, to the college and promoting its quality. Reward is at the heart of this, but it goes well beyond money. The rewards of the professional relate to the degree of independence, based on trust, he or she feels in carrying out the required role. Reward needs also to be a dynamic concept: extra effort and extra achievement need to be recognised in either money and/or other benefits. Reward should be seen to relate to achievements; it is no longer sufficient simply to plod through a long scale with yearly increments.

Although some clerical and manual staff may not currently relate to these professional ideals, the goal of one staff needs to be kept in view. Identification with the college, and the knowledge that effort and achievement will be rewarded, will bring all staff together. For many staff this will mean demonstrating that the apparent protection of conditions of service offered by national agreements may not be as valuable as the opportunity to benefit from local arrangements for development and associated rewards. Increasingly, however, local arrangements will supplement national ones, and may offer a way forward in the context of future pay constraints likely to be imposed by government.

The lecturers' contract

Lecturing and management spine staff are likely to be the major component of most colleges' staff and staffing budgets. To our customers, lecturers and academic managers are key first-line deliverers of the college's products and services. Clearly financial and other support staff are always required, but without a strong portfolio ably delivered, no amount of financial management and support to the process will create success. Clearly the best model is one of interdependence and the 'one staff' ethos. It is, however, because of their particular professional role and the historical assumptions attached to it, that the lecturers' contract has received special attention.

The challenge is to develop new contractual relationships under incorporation which retain the motivation of professional status, but enable the new culture of flexibility and reward for effort to grow.

Perhaps the first issue is that of class contact. The root of this concept, of course, was the traditional view of a lecturer delivering lectures, and needing a certain amount of preparation and marking time. Over the years, many other duties, including administrative ones, have been added, but there is ambiguity over what counts as class contact. The issue is that working on the basis of class contact assumes that some form of presentation to a class is the professional norm. In fact, presentations to groups of students is only one of many strategies. Nowadays the tutor is just as likely to be taking other sessions and duties such as one-to-one guidance, small groups, large lecture meetings, designing and producing materials, assessing and testing of all kinds, and a wide variety of other activities which could be termed facilitation of learning. With the introduction of National Vocational Qualifications (NVQs), the increasing need to work on employers' premises, and various forms of independent and experiential learning, the variety and complexity of the lecturer's role has grown.

The Silver Book, however, effectively establishes norms for workload, based on quite different assumptions. The 'correct' loading for a lecturer, for example, is seen as 21 hours per week class contact; senior lecturers are deemed to undertake other duties besides lecturing, and therefore generally have a workload of 18 hours. These figures have not been arrived at by careful analysis. Rather, they represent the outcomes of collective bargaining. They do not relate to changes in the lecturer's role, or to the influence of new technology which aids and assists the production and delivery of learning materials and activities.

It is interesting to note that up to the mid-1970s there was an assistant lecturer grade deemed capable of delivering 24 hours per week contact. This, of course, was in the age of the spirit duplicator or Banda machine; nowadays the photocopier is ubiquitous, and tools such as DTP, video and resource-based learning are widely available.

The point is not that class contact hours are too short, but that a re-examination is required of the total mix of duties. We need to establish a new culture built on carrying out a full professional role. It seems unlikely that lecturers will attain proper professional recognition until this ideal is embraced by all concerned.

Similar issues also arise from the length of the working week and the academic year. Both conform to a view of traditional academic terms during which intense lecturing activity takes place, followed by relatively fallow periods of recuperation, research, etc.: very few lecturers operate such a pattern. These norms are in any case at variance with the creation of a year-round service to their communities which many colleges are striving to provide. Once again, the challenge is not to increase working hours, but to create a proper professional contract which recognises commitment throughout the week and year, and does not elevate classroom performance of a traditional lecturing kind to prime importance over all other roles.

The issue of the lecturers' contract raises the difficult issue of what exactly a lecturer's duties should be. Lecturers have traditionally performed a wide range of roles connected with teaching and learning. As the days of duplicated notes and chalkboards have given way to competence-based learning and use of various learning technologies, lecturers not only manage learning, but write and copy materials, handle the complex assessment requirements of NVQs, and generally perform administrative functions. Most lecturers will acknowledge being caught up in these kinds of administration which, while essential, may detract from a focus on nurturing individuals' learning. Rather than allow this to happen to professional educators, it is necessary to recognise other specialisms and create administrative support staff of an equally professional kind. Professional support staff will repay investment by freeing up the more highly paid lecturing staff to focus on managing learning.

A similar argument for increasing specialisation applies to the distinction between managing and nurturing individuals' learning, and providing instruction in practical skills. In many skill areas there are highly able practitioners who can demonstrate the skills of brickwork, catering, machining, etc. This is separate from the professional role of planning learning programmes, coaching an individual, devising graded assessments, etc. Once again by recognising this specialisation, the contribution of both can be valued and made part of the learning process.

This theme of greater specialisation with its associated benefits of greater professionalisation and possibilities for diversification of individuals' patterns of work and remuneration, also applies to the management of the college. In further education, just as until recently in higher education, management roles have with a few exceptions been filled by academic staff. The issue of good teachers promoted to be poor managers has long been recognised. The introduction of the management spine was an attempt to recognise primarily non-teaching roles within national conditions designed for lecturing staff. Clearly many staff fulfilling a management role do so extremely well and have undertaken the training needed. Nevertheless, this tradition of looking primarily to academic staff to perform management roles has perpetuated the view that managing is not a specialism in its own right, but something anyone can turn his or her hand to. Incorporation has highlighted this issue. Colleges now need management professionals in finance, human resources, marketing and estate management. Many are looking outside the academic ranks to find them. Once again the issue is not that academic staff are automatically unsuited to management roles, which is manifestly untrue, it is that these roles must be filled by properly trained and qualified staff, whatever their origins, not by staff who are attempting to grow into the role.

Clearly such developments bring with them certain tensions. Academic staff may feel displaced or devalued by the introduction of new management specialisms. This can lead to a desire to cling to the more traditional professional identity based on academic excellence rather than a practical proficiency in promoting learning. Ironically, it can also lead to attempts to preserve academic conditions of service as a 'mark of distinction' and separate from the new managers. Change as profound as that represented by incorporation is impossible without tensions as roles change. The worst scenario however is of opposing groups of staff each trying to preserve status and privileges as they see them. This is why meeting the professional ethic, and rooting it in patterns of individual reward is so vital. The message must be that it is not to which group a member of staff belongs that matters, but the excellence, dedication and professional integrity of his or her contribution.

Towards a professional reward structure

All the points discussed above involve issues of pay determination, and its relation to the scope and intensity of work. I have avoided commenting on the positions of the trades unions (particularly NATFHE), since policy is continuously unfolding, and remarks both for and against any particular position, can easily be misinterpreted. Nothing argued in this chapter, however, should be taken as necessarily antipathetic to a trade union perspective. The challenge is to create a more highly-paid and valued profession operating in prosperous institutions. This applies whether an individual's remuneration is linked to personal performance or performance of the college as a whole.

In much of private industry, the annual employee pay review is well established and enables pay to be clearly linked to the prosperity of the organisation. Conventional wisdom would suggest that since colleges are not operating in the private sector as profit-making businesses, it is not appropriate for staff pay to be handled in this way. This view has produced national pay bargaining arrangements and long incremental scales up which progress is made annually with no reference to the health of a particular college. The management spine has limited this by providing only four incremental points, and principals' salaries have been negotiated in broad pay-bands.

The Further and Higher Education Act 1992, however, significantly changed the context in which colleges operate. Earning income, whether from the FE Funding Council, TECs or employers, is at the heart of the enterprise. Colleges now operate a profit and loss account, and are required to observe strict financial probity. Other ways of generating income such as property deals are also possible. Managers in this situation are very like their counterparts in the private sector. Together with the chief executive, they are clearly responsible for the financial health and on-going prosperity of the college. If marketing is ineffective, student numbers fall and financial losses accrue, they are directly responsible. Quite clearly, new arrangements for remuneration are not only logical, but necessary.

In essence, colleges will now face all the issues of maintaining productivity, improving quality, delighting the customer, and managing money which management theory has been addressing for the private sector. It would be a lost opportunity if the area of human resource management which deals with performance management was to be neglected. Many managers in FE have been learning already how to apply the work of authors like Peters and Waterman in **In search of excellence** (1982), and many others who try to provide tools for successful management. Much of this work focuses on how the performance of individual employees is nurtured, supported and trained for effectiveness and excellence. Its lessons will now need to be carefully examined.

The immediate harbinger of change is perhaps the provision in the new college instruments and articles of government for the salaries of the chief executive and designated senior staff to be agreed directly by members of the corporation. Properly managed, this could be the beginning of all management staff having a personal contract and spot salary, reviewed and updated annually. It will be for individual colleges to decide whether salary increases are based on some measure of individual or institutional performance. Both provide opportunities and difficulties to enable people to experience the direct relationship between their own performance and the fortunes of the college.

The link between pay and individual performance raises the issue of whether there could or should be a link between staff appraisal and pay. Conventional wisdom, in this case supported by some management theorists such as W Edwards Deming (1988), suggests that appraisal should be a general review of performance, leading to training and development opportunities for the individual, and/or developments in systems and work practices which can aid performance. A link with pay is seen as likely to turn an opportunity for meaningful dialogue leading to individual development into a pay-bargaining session. Clearly, uninhibited feedback and genuine dialogue are important, and not to be compromised. The challenge, however, is to find ways of recognising exceptional performance which clearly relate to the enrichment of the college.

For this reason, an element of performance-related pay (PRP) may be important. It would acknowledge not that pay should rise and fall in relation to the minutiae of performance, but that demonstrable striving for excellence is valued in what is still the most tangible way possible. In the author's own case, an element representing about four per cent of total pay is an annual variable PRP bonus. This seems to work well for all colleagues who are involved. It is not overbalanced, yet very clearly recognises performance related to discreet objectives, over and above the general operational management required. In some cases, a link between pay and performance can be even more direct. A marketing manager employed to increase income from cost-recovery courses could be paid a bonus based on a percentage of additional income secured.

PRP as an additional or bonus element is an unexceptional part of remuneration. In essence it replaces the automatic annual increment, and so must be budgeted for. However, PRP has attracted a good deal of criticism, partly due to the difficulties attending its introduction in the private sector. Part of the problem is that the concept has been applied in a variety of ways, some of which involved open-ended commitment to increase pay with performance. Clearly a key factor is the proportion of total pay involved. Experience suggests this should be kept reasonably small, but enough to represent a realistic reward.

Perhaps more difficult in the context of education and training, is the issue of measuring performance. The key question is 'what can the individual member of staff reasonably be held accountable for?'. Clearly the products of most employees' work, whether successful students, a balanced budget, a comprehensive strategic plan, involve the efforts of many. Once again, moderation seems sensible. PRP needs to be related to a fairly small number of clear objectives which are broad enough not to require an extensive process of counting and measuring. Where a particular employee is formally responsible for a product such as a plan, a group of qualified students, a set of learning materials, it seems reasonable that this should form the basis of his or her PRP. Part of what is being rewarded is obviously not simply the product but the successful process of facilitating others to work together in its achievement.

In summary, the combination of spot salaries, annual pay reviews and PRP could lay the foundations for a new culture of building excellence and rewarding achievement. It would be unfortunate if opposition to PRP destroyed what is almost certainly the only way for the foreseeable future that individuals' salaries can rise in relation not just to the cost of living, but to greater intensity of work. At the time of writing, the Government is operating what amounts to a pay-freeze in the public sector. This only raises the urgency of developing sensible, workable PRP schemes.

While pay is the cornerstone of any remuneration policy, non-pay benefits are particularly under-utilised in FE. The private sector has long recognised the value placed on company cars, private medical insurance, preferential mortgages and so on. Their value fluctuates according to the particular tax regime in force. Nevertheless, they are one way of bringing recognition and status as a form of value-added pay. The new FE corporations will wish to explore how they can be used within an overall structure of performance management. Beyond these large, and relatively expensive, items are a host of other possibilities. Some management theorists advocate incentive schemes ranging from share options to weekend breaks in Paris. Clearly there is scope to explore this in education, especially when pay is held down by government dictat. A particularly good discussion of non-pay benefits is in **Teaching the elephant to dance** by James Belasco (1992).

One objection I have heard raised to some non-pay benefits such as prizes, lunches, small gifts, etc., is that they encourage employees to look for a reward, rather than the traditional practice of expending maximum effort out of a sense of duty. This might be called the Florence Nightingale school of thought. While based on a puritanical valuing of duty, it ends up exploiting those who do make the effort required because they receive nothing more than those who do not.

'Nightingalism' may have succeeded in raising the standards of nursing, but it has not led to a culture of highly-paid, highly-valued professional nurses renowned for their customer care. In truth, the costs of small rewards are low, and the effect on employees' esteem can be dramatic. How many chief executives would benefit from holding a lunch for outstanding employees every month? What could the benefits be from offering a free weekend break for two every term for outstanding performance? What might the effect be if the caretaker or meals supervisor won?

Clearly there is much to explore, but the point remains that identification between staff and college corporation, rather than the relatively anonymous local or central government, requires a carefully planned reward strategy. There is much to be done to devise and fine-tune such a process to ensure fairness and openness to all employees from senior managers to part-time support staff.

The future

One difficulty with writing about the future of FE is that change is happening at such a rapid pace that all predictions may be out-of-date in the time it takes to produce a printed book. Two key themes seem destined to endure: quality in products and services; and individual development of employees. These are also the bedrock of a new human resources culture which demands excellence, encourages individuals to achieve it, and rewards them for doing so. These themes, however, cannot be imposed as if college culture was currently a *tabula rasa*. They will necessarily emerge and grow alongside new employment and remuneration practices. Because these will be focused on freeing individual energies, within a culture of accountability, they will be as threatening as they are liberating. Indeed, exploiting the possibilities, without being overwhelmed by the threat to established patterns, will be a key cultural challenge.

At the time of writing, following the breakdown of national negotiations between NATFHE and the Colleges' Employers' Forum (CEF), the latter is assisting colleges to introduce a quite new contract of employment. Its definitive form simply sets a framework of 37 hours work per week, and 35 days holiday, plus statutory holidays, per year. The mix and nature of duties is considered a professional matter to be determined within each college.

The clear challenge for managers in FE is to move beyond focusing simply on the contract, to new possibilities of customer service, institutional excellence and personal development. These are more difficult, and more locally directed. They involve, despite the inevitable initial focus on lecturers, a conception of the organisation as a whole, valuing all its employees. The new culture is one of reliance on quality (in the wide sense in which I have used it above) rather than on an umbilical cord attached to local government. As in all change in employment practices, the highest standards of fairness and reasonableness must be observed if damaging litigation is to be avoided. Like so many other features of the new FE corporations, the new culture is needed now. There is no time to lose if FE is to become the prosperous professional service promised in this chapter.

References

Belasco, J A (1992) **Teaching the elephant to dance: empowering change in your organisation.** Century Business

Deming, W E (1988) **Out of the crisis: quality, productivity and competitive position.** Cambridge University Press

Neale, F (ed.) (1992) **The handbook of performance management.** Institute of Personnel Management

Peters, T J and R H Waterman (1982) **In search of excellence.** Harper & Row

Thompson, M (1992) Pay and performance: the employer experience. **IMS Report No. 218.** Institute of Manpower Studies

Thompson, M (1993) Pay and performance: the employee experience. **IMS Report No. 258.** Institute of Manpower Studies

Chapter 5: Recruitment and selection – the heart of the college

Helen Gilchrist

Incorporation has brought, in the wake of the avalanche of financial procedures and systems, a thorough and rigorous review of the personnel strategies of colleges: a refocusing on not just systems and procedures, but on colleges as employers in their own right. Perhaps if there is not the complete change in mindset concerning personnel that has been predicted to roll across the FE sector there is a personality change regarding the importance of the college's biggest recurrent asset, its existing and potential staff. Certainly human resource planning is a key element of the strategic planning process. The effective planning and deployment of human resources will be the lynchpin of learning and teaching strategies, of employer liaison, of curriculum development and of community response. Achievement of Nelson and Colne College's statement of purpose and aims depends on our staff. Our strategic plan includes a section of human resources, which recognises that the management and implementation of change can only happen through the effective use and development of human resources. In other words, human resource planning will contribute greatly to the success or otherwise of colleges.

The dual attributes of freedom and accountability in terms of recruitment and selection of staff rest in the hands of the board and chief executive. The bottom line is, of course, that all procedures and practices must comply with the relevant legislation and that sufficient evidence has been gathered to demonstrate conformity. However, the responsibilities of complying with legislation are only a part, albeit significant, of the much more fundamental process of choosing the right person for the job. What may become an area of debate is the potential dichotomy between the role of the board and that of the principal/chief executive. The principal will routinely have direct responsibility for all appointments, except senior postholders and heads of department or their equivalent. She or he may be actively involved in many of these appointments, particularly full-time and teaching posts. She or he will wish to ensure that adequate procedures are in place for other posts. However, the board may wish to make its own arrangements concerning appointments and will have the right to decide how rigidly it follows general college guidelines as laid down in the college's articles of government.

Equally as fascinating could be the changing attitude of corporations when viewing human resource planning and management. The way in which the public sector has traditionally acted is very different from the way in which private organisations conduct their personnel policies and procedures. This is particularly highlighted in many recruitment and selection procedures and there is already some evidence that different approaches may be taking place for selecting senior postholders. Head-hunting or targeting potential candidates is still relatively uncommon in the further education sector. Salary negotiations do not normally take place. Psychometric testing is becoming more widespread but is still not common practice.

The recruitment and selection of staff for new corporations on whatever conditions of service mark a new stage in development as colleges determine not just the post required but the skills and qualities of employees. The whole process of recruitment and selection needs, therefore, to be reanalysed. Indeed, if one thinks that a member of staff is an asset for a longer period than most equipment, and in funding terms is potentially a long-term investment of say 30 years, rigorous thought to getting the right procedures should follow. Perhaps the clarity incorporation has brought on cost effectiveness will serve as a sharp reminder of the increasing dependence we will place on part-time staff who, in many senses, have been at the very end of personnel policies and procedures which colleges have formulated. Indeed, the growing role of support staff in their many guises – administration, technical support, general maintenance or learning support – should be reflected in the care taken over their appointment. All this necessitates training for any staff who will be involved in recruitment and selection. Perhaps a parallel here is to compare staff appointments with staff appraisal where thought has been placed on the need for appraiser training. A rolling programme of training and updating skills should take place for all staff and indeed board members. At Nelson and Colne College we have recently had a working group reviewing our recruitment and selection procedures. They suggested a number of refinements to our system and have put together a new training programme particularly related to issues of equality opportunity for interviewers. I would expect this to be updated by further training sessions, perhaps every two years.

In order to consider more fully the whole business of recruitment and selection I wish to look at three particular stages: post-identification, attracting interest, and selection and appointment.

Post-identification – defining what and why

We all know that the days of straightforward replacement of posts are well and truly gone and that many colleges have now established some fairly sophisticated ways of analysing and identifying requirements. There are, however, many more alternatives than previously existed or were seriously considered. Perhaps a post is identified. However, is it a teaching post or a post loosely defined as support? Can it be carried out not just more effectively but more appropriately by somebody on Administrative, Professional, Technical and Clerical (APT&C) conditions of service? There are also alternatives concerning the scale of the post: whether to use the management spine or not, how to equate the costs of the post against a cost analysis of the area of work. I predict that we will see an increase in the bottom end of the management spine posts to resurrect, in a very different guise, the area of responsibility which the former lecturer II post recognised. It seems to me that within the lecturers' structure this is one of a very few ways of exercising flexibility and acknowledging and valuing postholders who have significant sectional duties. Furthermore, incorporation has left a potential gap in the accurate and evaluated use of APT&C scales for support and administrative staff. Corporations can now choose to go outside, to continue to buy in to their authority's job evaluation scheme or to create their own. At Nelson and Colne College we are establishing our own job evaluation scheme with the help of the Advisory, Conciliation and Arbitration Service (ACAS). It has been an extremely time consuming but valuable exercise to attempt to objectively equate the wide range of duties performed by APT&C staff and the ACAS expertise has been invaluable.

At its most basic, a job description describes what the postholder needs to do to fill the identified post and most colleges have greatly improved this aspect of their recruitment and selection process so that they contain nothing too personal nor too detailed nor on the other hand too general. The changes in the Silver Book and a more rigorous approach to job description has meant that at Nelson and Colne College we have adopted a central framework of a standard job description for main grade lecturers which could act as a base for the vast majority of teaching posts. It will become more and more important that it is understood not to be cast in stone, that the job description is linked to staff appraisal and that new appointees appreciate fully the changing nature of their posts.

The personnel specification is the analysis of the skills, experience and qualities which the postholder needs in order to carry out the job description. This, and all other stages of recruitment and selection, must be embedded in the college's equality of opportunity policy and code of practice. The drawing up of a job description, personnel specification and interview procedures all have a direct impact upon who will apply and ultimately who will be successful. The whole process will have a direct impact upon the profile of staff within the organisation and the normal turnover of appointments during the year. If teaching and support staff are considered together, then there is potential for a considerable impact upon the culture of the organisation.

Finally, the attention with which we recruit part-time lecturers will, I suspect, be given more scrutiny as the demands of funding bring about a greater reliance upon part-time teachers across the curriculum. I would guess that although part-timers are part of all college curriculum areas, there will be changes in balance between full- and part-time staff, over different curriculum areas. No longer will it be chiefly the province of some vocational areas (hence a personnel specification) and the next stages of attracting interest and selection and appointment will be more carefully scrutinised for part-time posts than at present.

Attracting interest

Recruitment of staff always causes a swift look at the publicity budget and a re-appraisal of the press for insertion of adverts. Some colleges already ask applicants how they heard of the vacancy and I am sure that investigations concerning value for money will continue. Returning to equality of opportunity, it is an interesting exercise to register the gender and/or ethnicity of individuals asking for details of posts and then to compare them throughout the procedure until the final stage. As corporations, we will need to remember our obligation to attempt to recruit three per cent of disabled people to the college as a whole. It is our duty to advertise in the JobCentres. It is also of interest to look at other market research indicators, for instance, age profile and the confirmation or not of so called shortage areas, the number of applicants who apply regionally rather than nationally, the number of internal candidates, whether they are full- or part-time; are all useful indications concerning our recruitment and selection procedures. Looking into the future we will need, perhaps in those identified areas of skills shortages, to include a staff re-training package (looking for instance at the number of psychology posts advertised and what appears to be a scant number of strong applicants this could be a signal that the demand is outstripping existing qualified staff in this curriculum area).

It is fascinating to read the adverts from colleges in the Times Educational Supplement or Higher Educational Supplement every week. Here we are surely seeing the increasing phenomenon of competition within the corporate sector as each college tells us it is thriving, increasing its number of students and its student centredness (Nelson and Colne College included!). Whilst not wishing to pursue the analogy too seriously, it does remind me of holiday brochures and the moves taken against them to ensure that they comply with a reasonable Trades Description.

Has incorporation also generated the development of increased pay packages and other incentives to attract candidates in shortage areas? How does this square with the college's equality of opportunity policy and/or corporate view of the structure of the college? On a different tack, how many colleges also reflect their selling of programmes to adult students in the selling of their college to candidates? For instance, do we really provide for flexible working patterns rather than simply saying if you work in the evening you will receive compensation? Do we promote child care facilities? Do we give other indicators of what it means to be an employer who recognises family and home commitments? In short, how do we convince applicants, particularly in times of industrial anxieties, that we are a good employer?

Turning to issues relating to candidates for senior posts, it is clear from a quick survey of recent adverts that the use of consultants is increasing and that we have the potential of a two tier or track system taking place. Consultants, for instance, ask candidates about families, hobbies and concentrate on very different topics for closer scrutiny of individuals rather than use the same theme for all candidates. The use of consultants, particularly in the early stages of selection, sometimes mean that there is no continuity of individuals across the recruitment and selection procedure and that once they have weeded out applicants the rest is left to the board of the corporation. The corporation will, of necessity, be much more involved in senior postholder appointments than other staff and their views and practices may be very different, even at odds, with procedures and practices across the majority of appointments.

Finally, when we wish to attract interest as a potential employer we may in the future be wishing to stress re-training policies, our professional personnel section, our staff tutor, the social activities on offer at the organisation, the possibility of private health care, the flexibility of holiday entitlements, etc. This may well be done by some colleges not just to attract a better calibre of candidate but also to 'out-do' neighbouring, competitor colleges, furthering the ethos of competition which some principals and boards of corporations wish to foster.

Selection and appointment

It is essential to have clear criteria within the job description and personnel specification to enable accurate selection of candidates. It seems to me that the art of selecting appropriate candidates is to ensure that the personnel specification does not allow for criteria which are too general, otherwise it becomes extremely difficult to distinguish between a large number of candidates who could all fall into the category of possibles. On the other hand, there are dangers in being too specific, thereby excluding some individuals and reducing the potential pool of candidates, particularly if the college is attempting to attract non-traditional candidates. It is, therefore, vital that the personnel specification does not, by its very nature, exclude those whom it is trying to attract.

Once candidates are selected the interview procedure is the final test. In many ways this is the most imperfect science of all. The rigour of objectivity should continue during the interview session but, with a collection of individuals on the selection team and a different collection of individuals as candidates, it is very difficult to state with confidence that no subjective criteria will intrude. Nelson and Colne College has increased its use of tasks to test candidates' skills and expertise. It may be that secretarial staff are required to word process a particular document, or take dictation. Many lecturing post vacancies entail a mini teaching situation or a preparation of a particular topic. In other situations role play may be appropriate, for instance in the selection of a student support officer. For other posts a presentation may be the best means of looking at the strengths of candidates.

From the candidate's point of view it is important that she or he manages to obtain a feel of the organisation. Certainly candidates should be aware of the working conditions they may be expected to experience. In that sense, it is true that candidates should feel in some way part of a two way process, although the power usually lies on one side. In terms of quality improvement and critical self analysis it may be a useful exercise to give candidates a simple questionnaire to complete in order to ascertain the level of efficiency of the whole interviewing process.

The style of interviews reflects, in many ways, the culture of the organisation and particularly of the senior management team and/or principalship. There is no doubt that good interviewing means a rigorous approach to questioning and the ability to probe. In my view this does not, however, mean that it needs to be over aggressive or confrontational, particularly if the interview in question is a main grade lecturer post. At Nelson and Colne College we always give candidates an opportunity to either ask questions or make points which they feel they may not have had the chance to make to ensure that all candidates feel that they have had a reasonable chance to express themselves.

I am still surprised by the lack of direct use of the job description and personnel specification in applications particularly in the letter of application. In spite of the college making it explicit that candidates should refer to the criteria, this does not seem to be taken into account by all candidates. There is very little opportunity then for those candidates to get much further in their application if they have failed to address the essential criteria. Similarly I am occasionally appalled by the quality of the application. It may be our misfortune, but the college still occasionally receives letters on torn-off strips of paper or in handwriting that even the most patient interviewer cannot decipher. Applications do not have to be word processed or typed providing that the candidate's handwriting is clear and can be read.

On a technical note, corporations will have to take on board the cost of medical and police checks where appropriate, and as direct employers the importance of both of these is now heightened.

In our information sent out to all applicants we enclose Nelson and Colne College's statement of purpose and aims, our equality of opportunity statement and information concerning the fact that we are a no smoking college. At some point, either in the letter of application or the interview, it is a matter of rule that these policies are picked up.

The use of references does not differentiate between most candidates. Where they are useful is either in what they do not say concerning candidates who may be, for whatever reason, doubtful choices or outstanding candidates. It is sufficient in my view to check references when decisions have been reached at the interview stage. This differs once again with senior staff where references are taken up earlier on, and sometimes cross checked before shortlisting takes place.

Post-interview counselling is something the college offers but is wary of. Wherever possible it is preferable not to counsel unsuccessful candidates immediately after the interview when they could be in an emotional state. We consider it particularly important to counsel internal candidates, be they full- or part-time. In my view post-interview counselling also requires training for interviewers and should be treated with caution and consideration.

For the successful candidate there are technicalities such as ensuring that she or he is put on the payroll. There is then the more important aspect of induction which in a sense takes place during the interview procedure. Induction of new staff has been the focus of a working party at Nelson and Colne College and we have recently refined our procedures to include a formal monitoring system for all new postholders as well as a checklist of topics, some practical and others more general, in order to ensure that new postholders receive as much support as possible during their first year. I find it extremely useful to talk informally to new postholders on their arrival and then sometime towards the end of their first year in order to gauge their impressions of the college as well as highlight issues of concern or interest. Sometimes fresh eyes enable me to pick up things which may have been forgotten or simply not considered.

Issues

Colleges will have to consider very carefully not just the legal requirements of recruitment and selection but the integrity of the process and its appropriateness to the college strategic plan, in particular its human resource development. Amongst the issues to be addressed the following are important:

- the considered use of non-teaching staff;
- the use of grades and management spine;
- the merging of APT&C and management spine conditions of service;
- the balance between part-time and full-time staff and the consequent increase in attention to part-time staff;
- the flexible and changing role of the lecturer and how best to define it;
- the employment of staff between school and college and within the FE sector;
- the drift to regional applications and its effects;
- the tension between the corporate system and the search for the individual;
- the integration of management information systems within the personnel function;
- the introduction of a staff charter to attract and keep staff.

What I have outlined above and what I have described in this chapter relate to the concept of the corporation being a good and fair employer, where demands on staff are clearly described and expected and where any exchanging staff have a clear idea of their value and their place within the organisation. As colleges come under increasing pressure to account for their quality (**Assessing achievement**, FEFC 1993), to be accountable to their students (**The charter for further education**, DFE 1993), and to be accountable for the public use of money (**Funding learning** FEFC 1992), it is imperative that our new staff are not so weighed down by the responsibility of meeting performance indicators of a variety of shapes and sizes that their recruitment and selection becomes a matter of conformity to a prototype or checklist. The essence of appointing a valued member of staff is to recognise individual worth within the context of a corporate framework.

References

Department for Education (1993) **The charter for further education.** DFE

Further Education Funding Council (1992) **Funding learning.** FEFC

Further Education Funding Council (1993) Assessing achievement. **Circular 93/ 28.** FEFC.

Chapter 6: Appraisal

John Skitt

Introduction

This chapter takes as its premise that supportive and developmental appraisal of the performance of all staff, is a (if not the) major mechanism by which we can secure increasing effectiveness of our organisation. By effectiveness I mean the quality of the outcomes we achieve for our students and other 'clients' whoever they may be.

A primary focus of the examination will be to emphasise the importance of the *process* of appraisal. Other chapters explore the embedding of a professional development culture and the changing culture of human resource development. Both of these chapters are concerned with the context in which appraisal is developed. Where professional development is not an explicit institutional priority, nor reflected as such in the mission or aims of the institution, appraisal is unlikely to find a comfortable, or even tenable setting. To achieve the most from appraisal, there should also be commitment to managing change, continuous quality improvements and building quality teams. The process of managing and developing people demands an institutional network and culture that sets people at the centre of our thrusts and impetus.

Initially we may have some groundwork to do in convincing our colleagues that this is indeed a central or primary concern. Hence a main theme in introducing an appraisal process will be to build and instil confidence. Building that confidence will require attention to be given to:

- designing schemes;
- determining the elements of those schemes;
- creating the appropriate institutional context;
- who undertakes appraisals;

- improving our managerial competence;
- the role of the governors;
- the relationship of appraisal to Investors in People.

Designing appraisal schemes

Few colleges in the UK have had extensive experience of developing appraisal schemes. Their experience is certainly of value, but perhaps more from analysis of the processes that went into designing these schemes and in sharing the perceptions of those involved in doing so than from modelling subsequent schemes on the ones in use in those colleges. Any scheme should reflect the mission, objectives, ethos, culture, organisation and needs of those within the college. Hence no two schemes will be identical. It is particularly useful to explore how colleges with schemes already in place have sought to reflect those issues in their design. It may be worth asking the following questions:

- Have the principles and assumptions of the proposed scheme been agreed with staff?

- How have staff been made aware of those principles?

- Who is involved in designing the scheme? For what reasons? How were they determined?

- What part are the unions playing in the process?

- What are managers contributing to the process?

- How do governors see their role? How do others see their role?

- How is the embryonic appraisal scheme reflected in the strategic plan?

- What account is being taken of present arrangements for, and resourcing of, staff development?

- How is the scheme reflecting perceived strengths in the organisation's structure and processes?

- How are staff kept abreast of the development of the schemes?

Colleagues from many of the colleges who participated in the national pilot appraisal schemes or who, like Barnet College, had developed a systematic review process some years before, have been invited to share their experience with those colleges currently developing their own schemes. We are invariably questioned closely by all parties about the design process. That questioning has often proved very constructive in framing design mechanisms.

Elements of the scheme

Another area of keen attention is 'What makes up the scheme?' There is no one answer. Some colleges will favour very detailed schemes, which may be intentionally prescriptive. Others will establish a framework within which many approaches and styles co-exist. Both models have their attractions. The scheme should certainly provide for change and yet provide sufficient guidance to reduce uncertainty and confusion. Arrangements to encourage consistency in approach, to ensure confidentiality, to produce an agreed record, will often be of central concern to participants, especially in the early stages.

However, a very detailed document can be long, it may not be read or absorbed and can be a barrier or a source of wrangling. On the other hand, a concise statement of principles and expectations of the process can be accompanied by a set of appendices which addresses all the issues that will warrant people's attention.

The scheme itself may set out:

- the scope of the scheme, i.e. those to whom it applies;
- the existing organisational context and policies in which it is set;
- the appraisal cycle (e.g. two years) and timing of the process;
- who the appraisers are;
- a summary or framework of the process and the underlying principles;
- whether or not agreement is essential;
- whether or not it is a two way process;
- the range of activities which can be appraised;
- outcomes and arrangements for meeting identified needs.

Together the scheme and the appendices should reduce the concerns and anxieties, and answer the uncertainties and queries that will be encountered by appraisees and appraisers alike. (See **Figure 1** for an example of the issues that could be addressed in appendices.)

Figure 1: Suitable appendices to a staff appraisal policy document

Skills required of appraisers

Setting up and managing the interview

The interview process

Appraisal of senior staff

Teaching and task appraisal

Team appraisal

Identification of staff development needs

Training for appraisal

Implementation and monitoring

When things go wrong – complaints

Equal opportunities

Outcomes

Appraisal records

Appraisal and other procedures

Provision for part-time staff

Institutional review

Quality assurance

Source: Barnet College appraisal scheme

Creating the appropriate institutional context

I recall a former colleague entitling the opening chapter of a staff development handbook 'Getting started' (subsequently published in **Coombe Lodge Report** Vol 20 No 4). In many instances getting started will be the main hurdle. Any negative attitudes towards the institution, towards management, towards other colleagues can well come to prominence. Most unions who have members in FE are not against appraisal but they often have deep-seated concerns about the motivation of the government or those seen as its agents. Some will see appraisal as another unnecessary and heavy burden at a time of considerable change and upheaval. Many people will reflect on some of the fairly mechanistic schemes introduced in industry with mixed results and ponder whether those schemes should or could be adapted for FE.

Correct preparation for the introduction of an appraisal scheme is vital. An institution that is so disposed can reject whatever is offered. It is important for managers to demonstrate that appraisal builds upon and extends existing strengths in managing and developing people. These strengths may include, for example, known staff development policies and processes which are adhered to; effective equal opportunities policies; explicit selection and promotion criteria; comprehensive in-house training; annual review schemes; dedicated staff development or professional counselling staff. It is equally important to establish that appraisal is about evaluating performance, that although the appraisee is the central person in the process, it nevertheless provides a chance to reflect on the appraiser's performance. Above all it must be evident that assessments, outcomes and actions are implemented in a way that seeks to give support and provide for development. Where staff and managers alike are confident that the scheme is based on such assumptions, people will be more disposed to participating in the scheme. It is useful to recognise that appraisal will be threatening to staff because it is outside the experience of most.

The corollary is that management has the task of creating a climate in which an unknown and sensitive activity can take root and provide major benefits to all. Central to this will be ensuring that all stages of the design process are made known to all staff and that all staff have maximum opportunity to participate in the process or make comments. It will no doubt prove an impossible aim to achieve, but the commitment to trying to achieve it will be recognised.

Determining who the appraisers should be

This section considers who should appraise the body of staff, who should appraise managers (or those who themselves appraise others), and appraisal by students.

Settling on who is appropriate to appraise the body of staff depends on the overall objectives of the institution, who is responsible for achieving these objectives, the organisation's structure and the processes that underpin it. Associated matters such as managers' or appraisees' skills and understanding and the possibility of having managers in posts who are unlikely to be effective appraisers, should be borne in mind but should not pre-determine who appraises. Thorough training and a well thought out and understanding scheme can achieve much in a short time. In the longer-term it may well be essential to move managers who do not have the commitment, attitudes or skills to carry out the process effectively.

The national agreement on staff development, training and appraisal (between the the employers and NATFHE) recommends that appraisers should undertake no more than 10 appraisals a year. The national agreement does not, of course, provide for non-teaching staff. Many managers will have an increasing responsibility for staff on differing conditions of service and in the short-term at least, subject to different schemes, or possibly no schemes at all for non-teaching staff. Furthermore, many colleges will have a higher proportion of non-teaching staff, often working in larger or more clearly identifiable teams than was previously the case.

For other reasons too, the national agreement will require interpretation and adaptation in each institution. The college's strategic plan may place priority on the development of a particular programme; it may promote a particular organisational commitment, e.g. to flatten structures, 'open' management, continuous quality improvement. Those commitments may well be attainable through existing structures. However, they may not, and changes in the organisational pattern may be required that do not fit well with a 10 : 1 appraisee/ appraiser ratio. Organisations differ in their structures and this will be reflected in their line management arrangements. Our new responsibilities as employers add a further dimension to these organisational issues.

The number of people an appraiser appraises should be determined by what is most effective for our own college in the context of the issues identified above. Where it transpires that some or all senior managers have a larger appraisal load than is considered reasonable, it may be that their job description should be re-defined to take account of that for (presumably) the college must have a reason for the increased caseload.

Staff will make demands of and have high expectations of appraisers. It is therefore essential that appraisers can deliver on the basis of agreed outcomes. Appraisers must have credibility as appraisers, the skills to carry out the process, and the influence, seniority or authority to ensure outcomes are met. The smaller the number and the more senior the appraisers are, the more likely it is that these criteria are met. Another key issue for staff will be confidentiality; the greater the number of appraisers, the more difficult it could be to achieve confidence that confidentiality will be respected.

As schemes mature and become accepted, there may well be much more scope for delegating aspects of the process with the agreement of the appraisee. At Barnet, appraisal still rests with the senior management team of eight, after 10 years' experience of annual review and appraisal. The provision for delegation of aspects of the process has been accepted without much comment.

Appraising managers

While it is clearly important that managers should be appraised and determine who should do this, it is also necessary to ensure that colleagues at all levels are aware that such appraisal is taking place. Thus the scheme or its appendices should be just as explicit about the arrangements for the appraisal of senior staff as anyone else in the college. There is no reason why all managers other than the principal should not be appraised by the principal. The principal is responsible to the governing body for the overall management of the institution and for achieving the objectives within the strategic plan. It may be appropriate to delegate that task to a vice-principal in the case of some managers and there is of course an argument for managers having a say in choosing their appraiser. The appraisal of managers should explicitly recognise their managerial role and the nature of their tasks. The Barnet scheme has an appendix devoted to the appraisal of managers and their broad tasks are listed there.

Post-incorporation it is even more important that the governing body is involved in the appraisal of the principal (and probably the vice-principals). As the employer, the governing body has a responsibility to ensure that college management is implementing the objectives identified in the strategic plan and for keeping the overall management of the college under review. The governors determine the salaries of senior staff and in most cases that will include the element of performance related pay. The FEFC requires that the governing body establish a remuneration committee for the purposes of salary assessment. It is essential that the committee sets out the criteria for determining salary and the conditions on which performance is assessed.

Appraisal by the governing body should, however, be only one element in the appraisal of the principal. The principal has a close working relationship with other senior managers and is a key person for all the staff working in the college. How the principal undertakes his or her role has a major impact on the way the college works and the image it projects. Staff should have a role in the principal's appraisal. This can be achieved through an effective dialogue and a two way appraisal process where the principal gains honest feedback about his or her role. A more structured approach is to involve a representative group of senior management in the process. At Barnet, both methods have been employed at different times. Feedback from staff as a whole has been provided by the professional tutor, who has the role of staff mentor, counsellor and ombudsperson.

The principal has a key role in appraisal in another respect. Where the principal is seen to have a commitment to the process and undertakes that responsibility in a professional, sensitive and unrushed way it is likely to be reflected in the approach of and attention given by other staff.

Improving our managerial competence

Appraisal could and should be a key catalyst in assisting us to improve our managerial competence in all areas of the college's operation. Moreover, it demands a high level of managerial competence on the part of those responsible for appraisal.

The most credible appraisers will be those managers who are themselves considered by their colleagues to be effective and supportive. To achieve such recognition requires not only professional expertise and experience, but personal qualities of empathy, openness, frankness, recording, counselling and negotiating skills. Where those competencies are in evidence in the appraisal process it is likely that they will underlie the managerial style and approach in general.

Indeed, the college where the vast majority of those with managerial responsibilities possess such strengths, will be in a highly favoured position. The confidence will be there to manage in a direct, robust, self critical way and where the quest to improve quality is not inhibited by defensiveness and fudge.

The emphasis upon consultation, clear communication and an open, relaxed style by the FEFC in the early phases of its operation, serves as a useful lead to those of us managing institutions. There is another message, one that should be lodged firmly with the Department for Education and the Treasury – it is vital for the new sector to be built on a professional and sound approach to industrial relations in which staff are valued and have the proper representation of their interests by their unions. The main arena for that dialogue will be within the institution, within a framework set by the Colleges' Employers' Forum (CEF). That framework should be founded on recognised institutional managers' responsibilities in the field of industrial relations, and thus not create a climate which fosters management/staff conflict. The responsibilities of the unions are changing rapidly. The National Association of Teachers in Further and Higher Education (NATFHE) will need to examine carefully its own position and explore the value of linking with the non-teaching staffs' union UNISON. There will certainly be benefits to management and staff of having a single union representing the interests of all those within the college.

The role of the governors

Appraisal in colleges will be a new phenomenon for governors, although many industrial governors will have experienced appraisal schemes in their own workplace. The majority of those schemes will have been prescriptive and often pro-forma based. Many have also been primarily concerned with pay. Certainly it is important that governors' previous experience inform their involvement in appraisal in FE, although that experience should not be replicated.

Performance is at the heart of the appraisal process. The performance of those working in colleges is concerned with their contribution to the three-stage process the students go through in their college life, i.e. 'entry'; 'on programme' and 'exit'. Aspects of that contribution can be relatively easily assessed in qualitative terms; other aspects are less easy to qualify. The quality of learning rests in part on subjective matters. The process of appraisal should reflect that and governors should be conversant with and committed to the processes that will be most effective for the workforce and in achieving the institutional objectives.

The governing body should experience the appraisal process in the context of the college's personnel policy as it is only one of the policies or arrangements for which the governing body has responsibility. The personnel policy will include those activities shown in **Figure 2**.

The governing body's direct involvement in the appraisal process will be limited to the appraisal of the principal (and possibly other senior staff). Just as institutional managers can set the tone of the process for the college as a whole, so the governing body can create a positive climate, valuing of appraisal. Our governing body at Barnet College has actively supported the development of our annual review and latterly appraisal processes, without interfering with its development.

Figure 2: Aspects of a college personnel policy

1. Forward planning of staffing needs

2. Review of vacant posts

3. Identification of job description and the associated person specification

4. Recruitment procedures

5. Induction programmes

6. Annual reviews

7. Provision of staff development programmes to meet current and future needs both for the individual and the institution

8. Advice on industrial relations and health and safety

Appraisal and the Investors in People Standard

Colleges who seek recognition as an Investor in People (see Chapter 1) will need to give attention to the range of employer responsibilities relating to staff. The process of applying for recognition as an Investor in People is one way of raising staff awareness of people issues and of building college mechanisms which will in turn support an effective appraisal process. In order to satisfy the criteria, a college will need to demonstrate that its arrangements for appraisal extend to all staff, as does its provision for other aspects of supportive and effective human resource policies.

As colleges committed to change and the growth of our students, it is in our interests to be demonstrably committed to giving priority to the development and expertise of our staff to maintain and improve the quality of students' experience. Recognition as an Investor in People may well carry weight in the future in reflecting that commitment.

Conclusion

Many staff in FE have in the past had little or no systematic feedback on their professional activities. Many managers, it seems, were primarily concerned with numbers. It is not surprising that some of our colleagues 'got into a rut'. The result has been very sad and sometimes very wasteful for the individuals concerned and certainly for their students. Good appraisal can do much to ensure that does not continue. Appraisal can encourage and stimulate staff and provide real and lasting benefits to generations of students. Our aim should be to create an environment where staff regard appraisal as a valuable entitlement.

References and further reading

Duckett, Ian (1990) **Piloting appraisal: the Barnet College experience.** Barnet College

Duckett, Ian and Cynthia Lorne (1992) **Implementing appraisal: training modules.** Barnet College

Skitt, John and John Jennings (1987) A staff development handbook. **Coombe Lodge Report** Volume 20 Number 4. Blagdon, the Further Education Staff College

Chapter 7: For quality, against appraisal

Tony Henry

'You don't know much about this, do you?'

I had just been appraised by Sharon, a 17 year old black woman on a BTEC social care course. My problem was that I was not able to help her escape from a border she had created in Word in Windows (a word processing package). In fact it was the second time Sharon had been dissatisfied with my word processing teaching. In the second week of term she had complained about the fact that the template created for her course's curriculum vitae gave no prompt which allowed her to enter the fact that she had had two children. My fear is that Sharon may use the college's suggestions and complaints procedure next time so I have done a lot more preparation on escaping from borders and we have changed the offending template. Sharon's upward appraisal of her tutor is one that is replicated throughout East Birmingham College. The only appraisal which is worthwhile is that carried out by learners of tutors and tutors of their managers. While on the subject of the latter, my last appraisal by the whole staff showed graphically my weakness in not being there when needed. It also showed I was quite strong on vision. **Figure 1** shows the summary sheet of that appriasal.

> The wise leader does not make a show of holiness or pass out grades for good performance. That would create a climate of success and failure. Competition and jealousy follow.
> Lao Tzu

First of all I would like to apologise to readers for flitting between first-hand learning experiences and ancient Chinese philosophers. My only defence is that I find very little support for many of the ideas that follow in current educational theory and practice. Appraisal has become accepted by an educational establishment only too willing to ape the practices of industry and commerce just as those leading-edge companies in industry and commerce are beginning to ditch the

Figure 1: Summary of senior management's appraisal by other staff				
Position	*VP*	*Principal*	*VP*	*VP*
Approachability	212	241	266	278
Being there	270	190	251	283
Value added for students: *entry*	229	254	185	323
Value added for students: *progress*	223	259	202	278
Value added for students: *achievements*	231	269	191	278
Secure funding	241	320	254	230
External liaison	267	232	193	239
Gut reaction	183	277	234	268
Vision	246	339	195	251
Consistence	223	263	258	238
Intepersonal skills	195	242	248	267
Totals	*2520*	*2886*	*2477*	*2933*

practice. My central tenet is that appraisal of staff does not add to the quality of a student's learning experience and therefore the practice is a waste of time. There are other problems: an assumption that there is a connection between teaching and learning; the assumption that ritualistic practices such as appraisal and academic boards add to the quality of an organisation. At East Birmingham College we have never had any difficulty with either of these assumptions. No one believes that there is any necessary connection between teaching and learning. In fact our monitoring instruments show that as the teaching decreases on a programme so students are more successful. As for academic boards, we just got lucky. On the day the inaugural meeting of the newly constituted academic board was to take place three years ago it snowed. The board could not meet; more importantly, it could not set a date for its next meeting. Every day since then I have been going to work fearing a whole range of staff or student complaints about there not being an academic board – so far I have not received even one.

As I have stated earlier my governors, colleagues and I are alone in thinking this way and this has produced certain difficulties in maintaining an anti-appraisal stance. One interesting side issue is that the main lecturers' union, the National Association of Teachers in Further and Higher Education (NATFHE), originally took the position that they wanted appraisal because it was part of their national conditions of service. They believed that any erosion in this area may lead to further erosion particularly after incorporation. Another interesting stance has been that of the local authority which insisted that we follow the locally-devised appraisal scheme and when we refused, punished us by not allocating resources to support our home-grown alternatives to appraisal. I am looking forward to the correspondence later this year with the Secretary of State and with the Colleges' Employers' Forum when part of our budget is withheld as a result of not implementing an appraisal system. In fact the main reason I agreed to write this chapter was to rehearse the arguments that will be used in such correspondence.

So what sort of college would refuse to implement an appraisal system which most people believe in some way has an intrinsic link to quality improvement?

East Birmingham College last year had 7000 students (over 300,000 units); it operates on 15 different sites in East Birmingham. The wards of East Birmingham according to the Department of Environment **Z score** rank in the worst 2.5 per cent for deprivation in the United Kingdom. This score is based on the social variables of class, ethnicity, unemployment, overcrowding, lack of basic amenities, single parents and pensioners living alone. It is a very challenging environment and that is why it is populated by the best students and the best staff in the country. The students attend in spite of multiple disadvantages and no tradition of further or higher education. The staff work there because they are committed to redressing the social disadvantages of working and living in this part of inner city Birmingham. In spite of the difficulties, the college was registered to BS 5750 by the British Standards Institute in 1992 and was the subject of a very favourable HMI inspection about the same time. Student numbers at the college have doubled in the last five years and waiting lists are normal in our main curriculum areas. In short, the college is successful and that success has been achieved without any form of top-down appraisal.

Before outlining the case against appraisal in which I will be indebted largely to the work of Peter Scholtes of Joiner Associates, I would like to describe some facets of East Birmingham's organisation which make appraisal unnecessary.

The college exists for learners first, staff second and management a very poor third. Given these priorities three truths follow.

First, if learners are central to the organisation of the college then they must be the only appraisers. They are the main customers; they are the recipients of the service; they must be the only ones who can tell us how good that service is at the point of delivery. Learners at East Birmingham are involved in course team meetings and they also have access to a widely used suggestions and complaints procedure which is part of our quality system for BS 5750. They, their tutors and I are signatories to a learning agreement in which all parties promise to keep agreed standards during the learning programme. If the standards are broken by any of the parties then procedures are followed very rapidly to ensure that the mistakes do not happen again. The culture in East Birmingham is not one of apportioning blame but of making sure that systems are put in place to make sure that the mistake does not happen again. Deming (who died in December last year at the age of 93) reminds us that 94 per cent of everything that is wrong with an organisation is management's fault and so if there are problems it is at management level that they need to be put right.

Second, all staff at East Birmingham are organised in teams. These teams are given time from their weekly contract in the case of support staff or from their teaching timetable in the case of lecturers. Weekly meetings are held every Friday between 9.00 and 10.00. This practice has existed for five years. At first there was opposition: the cost (about £100,000); employers wouldn't like the start of teaching being delayed (not true); staff would not turn up (not true). All those arguments seem so hollow now compared with the advantages accrued by five years of team meetings. It is at such meetings real peer-group support (and non-support) happens. Staff and students work together on continuous quality improvement and the results show. The timetable of meetings is arranged so that support staff can join course teams every other week in order to give fresh views to academic staff and also to tie the curriculum into their thinking about their jobs. These quality teams are central to the quality improvement at the college and all they require is time. Lack of time together with lack of information, lack of innovation and honest wrong belief were the main obstacles to quality improvement identified by the Paul Revere Insurance Company in the book **Commit to quality** (1990). We have found at East Birmingham that all that staff need is time to develop their own particular approaches to quality; what they do not need is any form of appraisal imposed from without. What is also central to this system is the trusting, cherishing, honouring, prizing and loving of staff. None of these words appear in the Silver Book nor in any appraisal document that I have read but they do appear in the mission statements of many Japanese companies. They are also sentiments that run throughout Anita Roddick's book, **Body and soul** (1991). In it she talks about work 'opening the doors to her heart' and states: 'I think all business practices would improve immeasurably if they were guided by "feminine" principles – qualities like love and care and intuition'.

Third, management is an increasingly irrelevant and inappropriate way of describing the leadership of a college which is totally 'unmanageable'. In the last five years the senior management team of the college has been reduced by half; not a single student has complained. The savings in salary costs have been spent on environmental improvement and supporting the front line; again, not a single student has complained. The structure has been flattened to four levels: students; course teams; programme areas; principalship. Everybody at the college has a substantial teaching commitment. Members of the principalship teach an average of five hours a week; all other staff teach a minimum of 14 hours a week. It is this front-line experience which keeps the leadership in touch with the core business of the organisation – learning.

I feel that it is important to point out that the opposition to appraisal is not a soft liberal cop-out but is consistent with the quality philosophy of East Birmingham College. The college's chosen quality guru is Dr W Edwards Deming. In his book, **Out of the crisis** (1988), and in his lectures Deming insists that you must accept the whole of his philosophy; you cannot pick and chose those pieces with which you feel most comfortable. His 11th and 12th 'obligations' of management advise strongly against performance standards; his third 'deadly disease' is performance appraisal. Obviously one could interpret these as the aberrations of an old man approaching senility. However, in his recent lecture at the National Motor Cycle Museum, the 92 year old Deming was as fervent and as cogent as ever in his opposition to appraisal. As I mentioned earlier, the most coherent arguments against appraisal are to be found in the works of Joiner Associates in general and the essays of Peter R Scholtes in particular. Joiner Associates have been working in Madison, Wisconsin over the past 10 years or so to create a community-wide quality improvement network. Their efforts are best described in their publication **Quality in practice** (Joiner Associates 1987). Peter R Scholtes is a senior consultant with Joiner Associates and in his essay **An elaboration on Deming's teachings on performance appraisal** (1988) outlines the case against appraisal. In the next few paragraphs I shall try to summarise his views but I feel that the papers should be read and re-read to do them justice.

Scholtes describes the main elements of any performance appraisal system as being:

- a standard of measurement;
- a method of establishing the standard;
- a period of performance;
- a performance interview;
- a rating.

Performance evaluation has its own logic; it is straightforward, it is fair, it is increasingly accepted by staff. It can be used by both liberal and conservative managers. However, it is still wrong. In further education I have seen very little evidence that it enhances the learner's experience. Therefore we could spend all the time and effort required on other things. Appraisal is a distraction at best; a de-motivator at worst.

The first point that Scholtes raises against appraisal is that the work of any employee is tied to many systems and processes but performance evaluation focuses on individuals. Colleges of further education are volatile organisations. In the first week in September many of them have no students. By the third week in September 10,000 students may be following a variety of programmes on many different attendance patterns from basic literacy to degree level work. Such organisations are constantly changing and yet we expect to hold individuals or groups responsible for events, behaviours, circumstances and outcomes over which they have no control. 94 per cent of everything that is wrong with the system is management's fault and these issues need to be addressed in true Pareto fashion before wasting time and effort on the other six per cent.

The second point that Scholtes raises is that more and more employees are members of one or more work groups but a process of evaluating an individual requires a pretence that the individual is working alone. Performance evaluation encourages 'lone rangers' and is divisive. The quality team system at East Birmingham means that there has to be a new focus. Individual appraisal is totally inappropriate. Students and staff are jointly responsible for the success or otherwise of the learning programme. Such teams will be much more sensitive to the different experience, expertise and areas of competence of the team members. The requirements of the team will change from year to year if not from week to week. Teams will need to make judgements on a regular basis and these calls are much more central to the operation of continuous improvement than any appraisal system.

A third flaw with appraisal is that it assumes consistent, predictable systems but in further education these systems are subject to constant changes. Owing to the periods of time involved in appraisal whole new systems may be present from one appraisal to another. Performance appraisal is based on the pretence that the primary source of inconsistency or deviation from the standard is the individual employee and 94 per cent of everything that is wrong with an organisation is management's fault.

The final problem with appraisal is that it requires a process which is objective, consistent, dependable and fair. Scholtes starts his essay with a story from long ago:

> 1700 years ago the following observation was recorded about a man appointed to evaluate the performance of the imperial family in China's Wei dynasty: 'The Imperial Rater seldom rates men according to their merits, but always according to his likes and dislikes'.
> Scholtes 1988

There are a number of factors which can distort the evaluator's perceptions. These include *inter alia*:

- reliance on general perception of management;
- unconscious stereotyping and personal reaction;
- the tendency to rate around the midpoint or average;
- evaluator self-image as generous or tough.

In short, appraisal encourages mediocrity by rewarding those who set safe goals; it puts pressure on individuals to work around systems rather than improve them; it inevitably demoralises employees creating either cynics or losers.

A report from Her Majesty's Inspectorate 120 years ago considered introducing appraisal but it was rejected. The final sentence of the report says: 'In the game of mechanical contrivance the teacher will in the end beat us'.

Now, 120 years later, many companies are ditching appraisal because of an illness known as PASTRI (post-appraisal stress and tension related illness). When employees get a bad rating they do not feel like going to work owing to low self-esteem; when they get a good rating they do not feel like going to work because they know that all the problems in work in the organisation will end up on their desk because they have been identified as a stellar performer.

Finally, I would like to counter some of the arguments that supporters of appraisal make as to the positive nature of the process for the individual and the organisation. The first point is that appraisal provides positive feedback to employees and this is what is needed. If appraisal is the only source of such feedback then God help the organisation! There are hundreds of alternatives to appraisal for feedback. At East Birmingham every member of staff is entitled to a voluntary development interview with the principalship. Last year over 90 per cent of staff took up this offer. Any member of staff who is applying for a new post is entitled to a mock interview. Any member of staff who wishes to see me can book an appointment any day before 9.00 in the morning and I guarantee my presence. Most members of staff are sick and tired of the feedback they get from me as I wander around the college – I have no office and no desk.

It is also suggested that appraisal provides a basis for salary increases and promotion. Both uses are inappropriate. As stated earlier, capricious factors outside the control of the employee can effect any appraisal and any way, good performance in the present position is by no means an indicator of competence in the next position. It is sometimes argued that appraisal can give periodic direction to an employee's work and identify gaps in training and opportunities for development. Using appraisal this way is rather like McLuhan's warning about driving into the future with your eyes on the rear-view mirror. There are much more efficient ways of identifying organisational needs and individual needs than appraisal.

I must apologise again to readers if what has been said sounds too much like a ranting diatribe. However, when you are on your own and you want to be heard then sometimes shouting is the only way. After all a vision is something seen by you and not by others.

References

Deming, W Edwards (1988) **Out of the crisis: quality, productivity and competitive position.** Cambridge University Press

Joiner Associates (1987) **Quality in practice.** Madison, Wisconsin, USA

Roddick, Anita (1992) **Body and soul: how to succeed in business and change the world**. ISBN 0-09-175292-2 Vermillion

Scholtes, Peter R (1988) **An elaboration on Deming's teachings on performance appraisal**. Joiner Associates

Townsend, Patrick L and Joan E Gebhardt (1990) **Commit to quality**. ISBN 0-471-52018-7 Wiley

Chapter 8: Reward systems and management

Gill Brain

Reward systems and reward management feature frequently in discussions and thinking about human resource strategies but often overlooked is the opportunity to integrate thinking about rewards with overall strategic analysis and planning. Many reward systems rely on historical precedence and when probed can also be shown to be based on questionable assumptions and philosophies, particularly with regard to beliefs about workers' motivation. Indeed, different philosophies may be held by managers in different parts of the same organisation and thus conflicting signals and messages are often transmitted to people within the same organisation. Contradictions are also rife between different aims and objectives held by the same managers. In one breath managers may talk about valuing employees, about staff development, about Investors in People and total quality management (TQM), while on the other hand they discuss the budget in terms of increased productivity, forcing in new conditions of service, wage restraint and other financial measures which are likely to cause disaffected workers and increase the chances of industrial action. Contradictions are, of course, the raw material of management. Nevertheless, in many organisations the reward system is not thoroughly analysed; is an underused tool for improving performance and is not fully utilised to support strategic objectives. In the days when colleges had little control over rewards there was no incentive to explore and understand the issues fully. Since 1 April 1993 there has been a pressing need to move from conceiving of rewards in the former restricted way and recognising the part they play in the culture and strategy of the organisation. A key factor in unravelling the complexity is a greater understanding of staff motivation and staff involvement.

Staff motivation

While one member of staff suggests she would rather go to the gallows than agree to any change in her traditional contract of employment, another tells me 'give me some more money and I'll sign any contract you want.' Some staff tell me they would rather have time than money. Others, in spite of being relatively highly paid, show clear indications of lower job satisfaction than one might wish. What conclusions can I draw from this except that there is no easy answer?

Managerial assumptions about people's motivations, drives and interests are often based on home-spun psychology, or philosophies about human nature. Are employees self-motivated, driven by intrinsic rewards, or primarily interested in tangible, extrinsic rewards? My example above suggests both. Sometimes these assumptions are elevated to level of theories. These include economic theories which stress that motivation is driven by rational economic calculation; needs theories which suggest that work satisfies basic human needs; expectancy theories which link motivation to the expectations of employees about relationships between effort, pay and performance; and goal-setting theories which stress the importance of achievable, specific goals.

Taking an eclectic approach and assuming there is some truth in all the above theories, the research suggests that there are real benefits to be gained from incorporating the following design principles into a reward system:

Involvement

Reward systems are more likely to be successful if staff are involved in their development, consulted about their views and encouraged to develop a sense of commitment to the scheme. This includes consultation about the goals, targets and behaviour changes that will earn the rewards. A sense of involvement, or better still ownership, is likely to lead to a more successful system. Full discussion and understanding of changes could be linked in those colleges operating a TQM system to team involvement and goal setting. The complexity of motivational factors is a particularly potent reason for involving staff. It is almost impossible to predict the interplay of all the different motivational factors (financial and non-financial) which affect staff and can make or break a new reward package introduced into a particular situation. Research has shown that many new systems fail because the formal reward system introduced actually undermines an informal system that was operating for at least some individuals or sub-groups. In such a minefield of complexity, using the collective knowledge of the organisation and its people is more likely to produce an effective system.

Facilitation

It is advisable to try to remove unnecessary barriers that prevent employees being able to achieve high performance levels. In many institutions poor equipment, unrealistic time schedules, few support systems, lack of co-operation, and lack of clear communication networks prevent even the best intentioned staff from achieving their full potential. The result is likely to be disillusionment and demotivation.

Equity

Remuneration calculations and the performance standards on which they are based should be perceived to be equitable and comparable for all employees doing the same job in the same organisation. Apart from being a requirement linked closely with the demands of the Equal Pay Act, inequitable systems will have obvious demotivating effects. None of us, however senior our position, can resist looking at our colleagues and making comparisons. Finding we are paid less than others performing similar work is likely to foster a sense of being under-valued.

Reinforcement

Procedures should be in place to give employees reinforcement, encouragement, guidance and feedback to reflect their employer's interest in their performance and enable staff to see the direct link between reward and performance. Staff should be able to see that they can turn effort into performance and in turn earn desirable rewards. Many staff are underperforming because they are unclear as to what they should be doing. The incongruence between what their line managers are expecting from them, and what they think they should be doing might be resolved relatively painlessly by clear initial job descriptions, by regular review procedures and by higher levels of face-to-face communication at both formal and informal levels. The reinforcement procedures in many colleges operate counter to those which managers would actually claim to desire. The good, hard working, highly motivated staff get more and more work to do for little or no extra reward, while the not so good get given less and less to do but suffer no reduction in remuneration.

Relevance of the rewards

Time should be spent ascertaining that staff really are interested in earning the proposed rewards. While this may seem obvious for such rewards as pay, it is often not done for other rewards such as bonuses and benefits. Some of my staff tell me they would rather have more time than higher pay, others value holidays or security of tenure above monetary remuneration. They cannot, of course, always get what they want but it might be worth finding out what they want and examining all possibilities before coming to a decision.

Organisational effectiveness

While it is obvious that reward systems have a significant impact on the motivation of staff, they also influence other aspects of organisational effectiveness.

Organisational costs

Pay in most colleges will represent 75 to 80 per cent of all operating costs. By way of contrast labour costs in many other sectors are substantially lower. For example:

- Tate and Lyle 9.5 per cent;
- Laing Construction 15.2 per cent;
- Marks and Spencer 17.4 per cent;
- Post Office Counters 30.5 per cent;
- a shire county council 63.0 per cent.

The high costs of pay in FE colleges mean that there is less room for manoeuvre and in consequence some of the concepts found in general management studies of reward systems may be less applicable.

There is a huge challenge in the management of colleges (as with other service industries) of trying to contain or reduce staffing costs as a percentage of total costs, while at the same time keeping staff motivation, commitment and morale high since the delivery of the service depends so crucially upon their interaction with clients. A policy which gets this balance wrong may well end up cutting staff costs but also cutting staff morale such that the service is not effectively delivered.

Attraction, recruitment and retention of staff

In some areas (of both geographical and subject specialism) the rewards offered may be a crucial factor in staff recruitment. It remains to be seen whether this factor will lead in the medium- to long-term to a movement away from standard national pay and conditions of service. Not only will local labour market conditions have an effect here but also managerial style: do you strive for the very best staff or the best you can get? Do you want to create a permanent family of staff who stay with you or are you after the young, ambitious and restless? One of the principals whom I worked for in the early days of my career would say to new recruits at interview that he only wanted to appoint staff who would be moving on in about three years. In the expansionist climate of the 1960s he created a team of young, vigorous, innovative and ambitious staff for whom money was not the major immediate reward. They knew that their reward, if they proved themselves able, would be support in moving on to higher things. This is obviously not a philosophy that all would advocate, nor one that would work in all geographical areas or economic climates. However, it illustrates the influence of managerial style on perspectives of reward.

Organisational culture and structure

Reward systems also say something about values and can help to define and underpin a particular culture by contributing to such values as participation, entrepreneurialism, innovation, bureaucracy, paternalism, hierarchy, equality of opportunity. Does your reward system reflect an orientation towards people or competence? Towards a many-layered or de-layered structure? Towards conformity or initiative? Towards horizontal or vertical integration? Towards specialism or multi-skilling? Above all, does it really reflect your values whatever they are?

Organisational change

It follows from the above that organisations may sometimes be operating reward systems which actually conflict with or contradict the stated, official policies and strategies of their managers. While managers may claim to want staff with initiative and creativity, they may actually be rewarding conformity; where they claim to stress the importance of teaching and learning skills or of experience, they are rewarding those with degrees and higher qualifications; while they aim to create teams of equals, those same teams contain staff on a multitude of grades. At a time of rapid change such as we are experiencing in further education, and with traditional patterns of rewards which were developed for previous decades, it is more than ever likely that such incongruence occurs.

This may be particularly true if we examine the changing role of support staff in colleges. Traditionally, the distinction between teaching and support staff was strict and absolute. In the college of the past support staff were described in negative terms as non-teaching staff. They worked behind the scenes out of the public eye, and were often very low paid as a consequence of not being classified as highly skilled. It followed that many, with the exception of caretakers and chief administrative officers, were female, local and blocked from a career structure through which they could advance. The fact that many remained loyal and hard-working defeats most of the theories based on economic gain as the main motivator. I worked not long ago with a CAO who told me that his previous principal had told him that non-teaching staff should stay away from students – dealing with students was the job of the teaching staff only.

We have moved a long way from this perspective in a very short time. Support staff are now at the forefront in three fast-developing aspects of college life.

First, incorporation has led many colleges to employ a host of non-educational professionals at senior or middle management levels. Incorporation has accelerated the trend towards the employment of financial directors, accountants, human resources/personnel officers, premises managers, information systems specialists amongst others. Many of these new staff have no previous experience of FE and were never in the classroom, in contrast to the previously prevailing background of most FE managers. Their employment increases the general overall status and standing of the 'support' staff in colleges, recognises the important specialist skills and knowledge they bring, and offers a possible career structure for those who are prepared to seek staff development and training in future. Working as they increasingly do in finance teams, premises/accommodation teams, personnel teams, etc., even the most junior clerical workers in such teams gain a position, a specialism, a status, a potential future, not afforded to them previously.

The appointment of non-educationalists who nevertheless bring specialist, scarce and much needed skills into the organisation at fairly senior levels, has already begun to impact on the reward systems of some colleges. The pool in which we were fishing for traditional vice-principals was a known and controlled one in the past. The sea in which we seek financial, computer and personnel specialists is a very different one with less clear shores. The increasing trend towards using recruitment consultants in appointments adds to this drift into unknown waters.

A second change in the positioning of support staff in the colleges is the increased emphasis on a customer orientation. Whether fuelled by a TQM drive or not, few colleges have failed to change their perspective of the importance of the 'front of house' role of the telephonist, the receptionist, the payments clerk, the caretaker and many other support staff who deal daily and directly with the students and public, often at the critical threshold of the college and prior to contact with teaching staff. In recognising their key role, particularly in marketing and support service terms, colleges have begun a process of re-evaluating, training and resourcing such staff in a way which must eventually lead to changes in their reward systems if they have not already begun to do so.

Third, the growth of learner support services has led to the rapid development of hybrid posts which bridge the previous great divide between teaching and support staff. Support staff working in student services units, in open learning centres, in flexible learning workshops, with special needs students requiring extra support, with diagnostic and APL profiles, in NVQ competency testing, in libraries and learning resource areas, are often working directly with students to support and facilitate their learning experience. In many cases this has been double-edged. On the one hand it has shown how skilled such staff can be and how under-used they have been in the past. On the other hand it possibly demonstrates how wasteful we have been in using trained, professional teachers to undertake a plethora of tasks which do not make best use of their particular specialist training and skills. We must surely be moving towards the development of a team approach to learning with the professionally trained teacher as the manager of the learning situation and of a team of support staff (instructors, technicians, learning assistants – we have not yet devised the new terminology) who will contribute to the delivery of the total package or programme.

These examples alone will suffice, I hope, to demonstrate the difficulties of developing effective reward systems in the FE sector in its present state of flux. Particularly where, as is common in the UK, rewards have tended to be based on the kinds of jobs people do, evaluated by more or less systematic job evaluation processes, fundamental change in the nature and types of jobs in the colleges has led to some confusion. It is perhaps time to look more closely at alternatives to the traditional model.

Alternative perspectives

Two main alternative approaches have been used extensively in the private sector but rarely in the public sector. The first is altering the reward base used for assessment of rewards; the second, the use of the wealth of non-pay rewards which are available for use. The best new systems will possibly do both. Let us look at some current trends in business and industry and how these might apply in colleges.

Non-monetary rewards

Many organisations offer a wider spread of rewards than have not been traditionally utilised or exploited to the full in colleges. Even where colleges do offer a combination of some of the features below they rarely perceive or present them as a coherent staff package. At Salisbury College, for example, all staff are able to take any college course without payment but this was not defined as part of the reward system until recently. In monetary terms, for example, there are the possibilities of fringe benefits, perks, bonuses and performance related pay plus entitlements to the use of a creche, to free training, to health, pension, insurance or transport benefits. Non-financial benefits include interesting tasks, good social relationships, influence over decision-making, involvement in key issues, praise and recognition, training opportunities, job security, facilities at work, leisure time, flexible working time, job share opportunities. Rewards may contribute to staff feelings of being valued or security and peace of mind. The coherence of the whole package is important. A reward system designed to be team orientated is undermined if company cars and health care are based on individual status.

Local pay determination

There has been a trend away from prescriptive national pay systems towards local pay determinants. The reasons for this lie both in the market and in structural and organisational factors, particularly the principles of decentralisation into semi-autonomous business units or cost centres. So while the trend is also towards simplified pay systems, there are circumstances in which it is considered appropriate to allow differences in reward systems to reflect differences in work or job structure or to create a separate identity for a particular group, function or location. The situation in FE so far has not encouraged differentiation and national bargaining and scales of pay have predominated. There are signs that this is changing. Even before the recent moves towards a flexible, open ended contract for lecturing staff which will almost certainly precipitate differentiation depending on local interpretations and agreements, there were colleges who had begun to use different criteria for the remuneration of staff in particular units e.g. short course units, management/consultancy units, enterprise units, employment training units and so on.

Stimulated pay structures

There has been a clear movement recently towards simplification of pay structures. Systems which had not been kept under constant review have tended to drift towards increased complexity as ad hoc decisions pile one on another, creating new grades to solve particular problems. Such complexity is brought into clear focus when organisations undergo review and re-organisation. The trend towards de-layering has accelerated this move to simplification. A recent local authority re-organisation reduced 38 levels to just 12.

Non-traditional pay plans

Another trend has been the growth of interest in non-traditional pay plans. Although experimentation on this front has resulted in varying degrees of success there does seem to be a move away from traditional job-based remuneration, where the primary determinant of reward is the type of job held by the individual. Job-based remuneration emerged with industrialisation and is particularly suited to mass production, substituting for the output-based reward system which characterised pre-industrial society. Mass production achieved product standardisation and standardisation of task performance. The job became the basis for all human resource management with selection, training and motivation all directed towards achieving standardised task performance specified in standardised job descriptions. While variants of output-based pay remained (notably in piece work) in the main output or performance related pay was restricted to those jobs where the individual was clearly the major determinant of output, e.g. sales and management. The job-based orientation of the scientific management school of thinking has dominated the 20th century, powerfully influencing our perception of work. The concept of job ownership emerged and was expressed in the trade union movement through collective bargaining, job assignment viewed as a right, rules restricting performance to tasks specified in job descriptions, demarcation disputes, job evaluation techniques, and different wages for different jobs.

In contrast, a more recent desire to simplify complex reward systems and to promote greater flexibility and multi-skilling, has led to an increased interest in person-based systems and/or performance-based systems. Of these three main bases of remuneration systems, some new schemes have emphasised one base exclusively while other schemes use combinations. Thus one modification of a traditional job-based scheme is to re-categorise many previously distinct jobs into a few broad categories. In another instance members of a production team may receive the same reward but may perform any of the broad range of team tasks. Some forms retain a job-based primary structure but reduce this as a proportion of total pay and increase supplementary components based on skill or performance. A number of schemes have abandoned the job-based element and rely primarily on skill or performance. Some performance-related schemes emphasise group or team rather than individual performance. Profit sharing schemes may vary the profit unit used and gainsharing schemes provide payments according to labour cost savings instead of profit increases. All of these non-traditional approaches involve revised concepts away from job-based and towards person- and performance-based schemes as being more compatible with variable products, technology and flexible organisation.

Finally, an offshoot of the trend outlined above, is the move towards multiple pay plans recognising that the three bases for pay are not mutually exclusive and each is better suited to different situations. Maintaining a strategic distinction between the three and understanding the advantages and disadvantages of each does not prevent the design of an overall compensation programme which merges all three.

Output/performance-based rewards are better suited to individuals, teams or units where the relationship is approaching that of an independent contractor, where work is viewed as the production of outputs (not the performance of tasks), where output can be clearly defined and measured, and where achievement is significantly influenced by the employee with little need for additional supervision. (Classic examples include sales commission, executive performance, garment manufacture.)

Job-based compensation is suited to organisations characterised by bureaucracy, standardisation of products and tasks, employing routine technology in relatively stable conditions. (Classic examples include mass production manufacturing, administrative activities in routine services, e.g. insurance.)

Person-based systems are most compatible with work that is not easily defined in terms of specific and stable tasks, and where skill and knowledge constrain the tasks which can be performed. It is often therefore associated with career paths of advancing skill and pay linked with seniority and qualifications. (Classic examples include scientists, teachers, craftspersons.)

The shift from production of goods to the production of services, increased competition, instability and change, greater need for flexibility, responsiveness, innovation and co-operation, matrix organisations, project teams, quality control circles, have all contributed to demands for greater integration between reward systems and organisational strategy. The increased recognition of person- and output-related compensation provides the opportunity for greater customisation of pay plans to complement varying situations and strategies. Understanding the three different components provides for a better analysis of strategic options. It is possible that it will become increasingly common for a single employee to receive portions of compensation based on all three components and that the proportion provided by job-based pay will continue to decline in relation to the other two. For example a production/service task could be organised as a team assignment, all members of the team receiving the same job-based pay. Additionally, some members may receive higher rates as they improve the skills they contribute to the team, and team bonuses may be given related to performance goals which may change over time.

The teachers' role

Bearing in mind some of the above points, it is now surely time to take a fundamental look at the work of our teaching staff before we hurtle into hasty decisions which may take us where we do not wish to go.

In further education we have so far been reactive rather than proactive, over anxious perhaps to prove ourselves the 'new managers' well capable of rising to the challenges of incorporation and demands for increased productivity. Let us pause to reflect on our underpinning philosophy before we finally decide on the way ahead for the next decade or longer.

But before looking forward perhaps we should look back. Early work by Herzberg and others suggested that job enlargement usually led to job enrichment, thus the moves to flexible team approaches in some industries, notably Volvo. As an antidote to the devasting monotony of the typical production worker whose job had been based on the theories of Taylor (increased repetition led to increased efficiency), the job enlargement philosophy was certainly correct. Applied, however, to the current role of FE lecturer it has probably passed its sell-by date. Over the past 20 years we have ad hoc added to the role of lecturer that of learning facilitator/supporter, learning resource producer, information technology specialist, pastoral worker, marketeer, course/programme manager, deliverer of integrated core skills, raiser of European awareness, team worker, tester, assessor, examiner, deliverer of open/flexible/distance learning, administrator and increasingly manager. By anyone's standards this is surely exhausting rather than enriching. Have we analysed carefully before concluding that this is what we really want? Have we thought about the consequences for the lecturer, the student, the organisation, the profession? Have we compensated them highly enough for struggling to meet these enormous challenges often with no initial training in these multiple skills and little in-service training or support? On the contrary, I suggest we complain at their lack of flexibility and attempt to impose new conditions of service such that they work longer hours, for more weeks, with reduced remission. Before carrying on down this road we should surely examine our perspectives, analyse our position, and be absolutely sure that we want the probable consequences.

Two extreme models may help to highlight some issues:

1. If the FE lecturers' role continues its amoeba like growth, its parameters grow more uncertain and borderline disputes continue to increase due to heightened sensitivity to threats from potential rival groups such as technicians, instructors, administrators, clerical workers, counsellors, careers advisers. The professional status of lecturers is constantly being undermined. They are required to overstretch themselves, do everything themselves, or are threatened with the employment of others who will do it as well and cheaper.

   The role becomes confused, as the focus shifts arbitrarily between a job-based model defining the job in an indeterminant way based on often unclear job descriptions which include some vague skill-based criterion (degree preferable, industrial experience useful, teacher training an advantage), and threats about performance related remuneration although we are vague about outputs.

The undervaluing of staff, the low morale, the possible prolonged or intermittent union disputes all add fuel to the lowering public perception of teaching as a profession and it is consequently de-professionalised.

2. An alternative model is that we undertake a reappraisal of the role of the lecturer at this crucial point in the history of our profession. We clarify more precisely what we mean by the professional teacher, what skills, knowledge, activities, tasks, training and experience we require. I would hope that this process would produce a clear definition of the professional lecturer/teacher as a highly skilled manager of the learning process, whose training and experience enables them to understand and control the complexity of the learning situation and to manage a team of para-educationalists who assist in ensuring the right environment, resources and general instruction and assessment are available for students. In achieving this utopia we will have successfully:

   – contained the role creating fewer amorphous boundary problems;

   – professionalised the role, recognising a unique and complex combination of skills, knowledge and abilities that characterises the teacher;

   – enhanced the sense of self-worth and value of teachers by removing threats of de-skilling; and

   – re-established the prestige and status of teacher/lecturers in the eyes of the public, parents, employers, politicians and last but not least students.

As an organisation changes its direction, its priorities and a large part of its activities, it is almost certain that it will need to incorporate a new remuneration and reward system into its plans. For some colleges it may be that they continue to live with the inconsistencies and contradictions for as long as possible before reluctantly facing the inevitable. However, changing the remuneration system, if well managed, may help to bring about organisational change. The argument that it is better to wait until all the other changes have settled down first may well be to waste a good opportunity to realign strategy and reward systems in a coherent way. We may never get a better opportunity.

Chapter 9: HRM in the next decade – an external perspective

Jan Wagstaff

No man is an island entire of itself
John Donne

No employer is free from external influences, the public sector employer even less so. All human resource policies will be influenced by events outside the employer's control requiring changes which may or may not be in sympathy with the ethos of the organisation. Researching the external environment is one of the fundamentals of planning ahead but one that it is easy to overlook in the human resource management field. Indeed, in the past there has been little contribution at all to strategic plans from the human resource professional; the assumption seems to have been that staffing matters follow rather than contribute to strategic planning. There are now such major changes in employment matters arising from external sources that failure to take them into account during formulation of the strategic plans could seriously prejudice achievement of those plans.

If colleges are to develop appropriate strategies for managing their human resources over the next decade they must not be knocked off course by changes which could have been predicted. Forced change at relatively short notice usually equals additional cost, cost which could be minimised or turned into gain by better planning. Nor does the reactive approach of changing policies when forced to do so help maintain staff morale. Such swings of policy can be viewed suspiciously by a workforce uncertain and fearful about the future.

In the late 1980s at the annual vice-principals' conference I was rash enough to suggest some of the changes in employment matters that I saw having a major effect on college employment policies. These were:

- demographic issues;

- specific features of the labour market, for example, shortage of skills and professional labour, change in emphasis from recruitment to retention and development, changing patterns of employment, increased attention to equal opportunities in employment;

- importing techniques from the private sector such as different remuneration strategies and the decline in industry-wide bargaining, with moves to single table bargaining and harmonisation of terms and conditions;

- legislation, for example, the major influx of legislative changes particularly from Europe.

Three of these areas, demographic issues, labour market features and European legislation, are typical examples of external influences which colleges cannot change but can plan to take advantage of. This chapter explores these issues in some depth.

The importation of techniques from the private sector will no doubt continue apace but in general can be at the college's choosing. However, it is likely that external pressure from the fund holders and funding agencies will be placed on college managers and governors to introduce certain techniques. The mechanism of holding back a percentage of funding can be a powerful tool to persuade colleges to implement certain techniques or changes required by government.

Readers only have to look at the NHS trusts and the new university sector to draw their own conclusions about new techniques. Performance related pay is rife in the trusts and growing rapidly in the new university sector; national collective bargaining is weakening and there is talk (if not action) everywhere about harmonising terms and conditions.

The key in adopting approaches from other organisational forms is that they should be appropriate to assist the achievement of the college's objectives. There are fashionable techniques which have failed in the private sector and are now being abandoned. It would be a great pity if we did not learn from this but continue to introduce practices which we can be fairly sure will lead to failure for us also.

It is probable that other techniques will be adopted with enthusiasm in the future, maybe the cafeteria system of remuneration, and almost certainly the concept of full performance management. Perhaps single union colleges and no industrial action deals is too much star gazing!

Demographic trends and their effect on employment policies

It is something of a contradiction to talk of shortage of labour at a time of recession, considerable unemployment and many colleges making staff redundant. However, a brief look at the predictions for the labour market in the middle and late 1990s and the early part of the next century reveal that labour shortages are still very much an anticipated problem.

It is forecast that by the year 2000 the required workforce in this country will have increased by one million, but only half a million extra people will be available for work. The number of young people in the UK available for work is forecast to drop by a third in the early 1990s and to continue to drop into the 21st century. This will have a knock-on effect on the numbers of and demands for older recruits.

Similar patterns are reflected in most European countries. The total populations of Italy and Germany are expected to be lower in 2020 than in 1985 with a 38 per cent drop in Italian 15 to 24 year olds. France is expected to show a similar drop in 15 to 24 year olds even though the general population will continue to grow.

Demand for employees is expected to rise worldwide with the assumption that world recession will (may?) end in the late 1990s. In Europe the forecast is optimistic with the Cecchini report predicting an overall increase of 1.8 million jobs as a result of the single European market alone but predicting a loss of half a million jobs in the period 1993 to 1995.

Forecasts of economic activity are notoriously unreliable but forecasts of the supply of labour are perhaps a little more certain. Whatever overall shortage materialises it is predicted that the shortages will vary dramatically between employment groups. The shortage of quality employees is predicted to be particularly apparent in managerial, professional and technical areas, three areas of significance for colleges.

These potential shortages of quality recruits, when set against a background of rapid change in curriculum, rapid change in organisational tasks and great need for flexibility and diversity in our staff, are likely to have a major impact on our approach to recruitment and selection. The emphasis will move to human resource/ succession planning and developing internal talent in a structured way.

Greater competition from industry and other colleges, no longer bound by national terms and conditions, for this highly trained and skilled workforce may mean that we have to look at the concept of retention packages in the way we looked at attraction packages in the 1980s.

The use of individual contracts negotiated to suit employer and employee will surely grow. We may even move towards the Japanese model where a small, highly paid professional core of staff is augmented by people contracted to achieve specific short-term goals.

At a time of labour shortages equal opportunities becomes more a matter of self interest for the employer than one of altruism. Whilst this may not be the case in the education sector there will an added incentive for colleges to improve their attractiveness to minority groups.

An equally pragmatic impact on progress for equal opportunities will be the major shifts in employment legislation. There is also evidence that there is a little movement in values in some fields of employment towards equality of opportunity. The recent report commissioned by the Bar Council (unpublished) is encouraging, for whilst it revealed much discrimination, the sheer existence of the report is a significant move forward in a very traditional profession.

The combination of labour shortages, major shifts in employment legislation and some move in values should lead to the employment of a workforce more representative of the whole population. Colleges, although committed to equal opportunities on a value basis, do not always follow through with practical policies. The employment policies on working patterns, sabbaticals, career breaks, job shares, etc., must change and not lag behind need if we are to attract and retain high quality employees.

Effective ways of managing the long-term employee must also be found such that flexibility and job changes become important, respected and rewarded. The current view that promotion is the only success route and the only vehicle to attract additional rewards will need to change.

The influence of legislation and the European Community

Legislation is a major external force on the way employers run their businesses; at best the employer plans for and changes policies to comply in a positive way, or, at worst pays the penalty for non-compliance when brought to account. It is useful to reflect that the law represents the minimum standards an employer should comply with, the good employer will have policies of a higher standard.

The attitude to and usage of legal processes in employment has shown a considerable shift in recent years. There is a greater general awareness of the employment rights of employees and a greater willingness to challenge alleged failures to comply. Trade unions in particular have overcome their reluctance to use the processes of law and are taking both collective and individual challenges through the tribunals and courts with considerable success.

The proactive employer will scan the legal environment when making strategic plans. There is at least some certainty in this forward planning as legislation is framed and published some years before its final implementation date. This is particularly pertinent in employment law as many of the changes are due to European Directives which are introduced with a due date for adoption, often two years in the future. The approved Directive will have been preceded by a well publicised draft for up to two years enabling some tentative planning to take place.

UK and European legislation are to some extent pulling in different directions; UK legislation favouring deregulation for employers and European legislation seeking to set a legal climate of employment rights intended to harmonise conditions across the Community.

All member states on joining the Community accept the supremacy of European law and the European Court of Justice (ECJ) as the supreme court, so eventually the UK will move towards the European approach.

Much of the drive for improved employment rights comes from the Single European Act 1986, to which the UK was a signatory, and not from the Social Chapter. The Maastricht Treaty, with its limited opt-out clauses for the UK, will not affect the current and medium-term waves of legislation.

The Single European Act (SEA) introduced the concept of free movement of goods, services and people within the market. For competition to be fair organisations should, to quote a popular phrase of the day, 'operate from a level playing field'. In employment terms this means harmonisation of employment rights for employees across the Community. Thus the flood of EEC Directives coming into force now and over the next few years is aimed at this harmonisation.

It is the Council of Ministers, not the European Parliament or Commission, who finally decide what the European Directives shall be. However, the SEA introduced the concept of qualified majority voting for many matters so that one member state alone can no longer veto a proposed law. The UK is not alone in having to implement statutes its government is not in agreement with.

We can expect to see, therefore, a legislative climate which reflects many of the principles of the Social Charter (and maybe the Social Chapter) though based on the SEA.

These principles are:

- free movement of workers within the Community;
- fair remuneration for employment;
- improvement of conditions of employment;
- social security;
- freedom of association and collective bargaining;
- vocational training for all employees;
- equal treatment for men and women;
- information, consultation and participation arrangements;
- improved health and safety standards.

Most of these probably sit comfortably with the notion of a good employer, but notions and practice are still far apart even in the education sector.

The special relationship between the public sector employer and European legislation

All employers in the UK are going to have to change some of their employment policies if they are to remain within the law. Public sector employers will have to do it earlier and to a greater degree.

The mechanism for implementing the Directives in member states is via their own legislative processes; the Directive gives a due date by which member states should have their own laws on the statute book. The UK has a variable record in bringing in the requirements of the Directives on time and an equally variable record in bringing them in in entirety.

An article in the original Treaty of Rome specifies that a member state 'may not profit by its own failure' to implement a Directive. Failure to bring in an employment Directive would, as the state is an employer, allow the state to profit by its failure. Hence, where Directives have not been implemented either on the due date or in their entirety, the state's employees are covered by the 'unconditional and sufficiently precise provisions of the Directive'. This is known as vertical direct effect, i.e. public sector employers (not just the state) have to abide by the Directive regardless of the form of its own state's law. This usually means compliance with change at an earlier date or to a greater degree. The Foster v British Gas case in 1990, and several subsequent cases, established that the definition of public sector employment covers the education sector even after incorporation.

The delay in bringing in Directives produces two types of employers and employees, the private sector not affected until the Directive is implemented fully into UK law, and the public sector affected on the due date. However, this time lag may become a feature of the past. A recent case in the ECJ, Francovitch v Italian Republic (1991) will encourage governments to implement Directives on time and at the correct level. This case has established the principle that any employees, private or public sector, can sue the state for compensation if they have suffered loss as a result of the state's failure to incorporate the full provisions of a Directive into state law. This case could have interesting implications post-incorporation if all the rights of the Acquired Rights Directive are not adhered to.

It is extremely important that college managers fully investigate the changes in employment policies that existing and new Directives will require and plan for them in a structured way.

Directives of particular importance

Much attention is focused on the Directives concerning health and safety at present and there are many more in the pipeline. But what will have a more significant impact on the management and development of people are the Directives on equal treatment and the way in which the ECJ is interpreting them, and the Directive on maternity provisions. Of lesser significance, but still important, will be the effects of the Working Time Directive and the Competition Distortion Directive.

The Directives on equal treatment, 75/117/EEC and 76/207/EEC (gender only – race and disability are not covered), have existed since 1975 and 1976 and the UK statutes, Sex Discrimination Act and the Equal Pay Act, have been amended towards compliance.

There has recently been an increase in appeals based on these Directives to the ECJ from all over the community and a distinct theme in the ECJ rulings. All such rulings of course create precedent for the UK and have in effect changed significant aspects of the interpretation of our discrimination legislation.

The present rulings are based on the concept that: unlawful discrimination occurs when there is an application of different rules to different groups such that there is a disproportionate effect on the sexes, which cannot be justified and the effect is to the detriment of the less favourably treated group.

Women form over 80 per cent of the part-time work force in most European countries (85 per cent in the UK), a very different ratio from the full-time work force and hence the ECJ has ruled that differing terms and conditions of employment for part-time employees which cannot be justified will be seen as discriminatory.

It is not easy to justify why part-time staff should be treated differently from full-time staff and recent cases have established the rights of part-time staff to:

- salary progression based on length of service according to the same rules as for full-time staff;

- equal treatment for payment for attendance at training courses;

- equal treatment for severance payments on reaching retirement age (the Directive on occupational social security requires equal access to pension schemes for men and women); and

- equal treatment in relation to sick pay.

The principles established by these judgements can be extended to all employment policies which result in differential treatment for part-time staff.

It is hoped that these judgements will encourage college managers to undertake the long overdue revue of how part-time staff are used and rewarded.

In March 1994, the House of Lords, in a series of rulings, changed the employment status of part-time employees. Unfair dismissal and redundancy laws breach European equality laws by discriminating against part-time workers. The government will now have to amend the Employment Protection (Consolidation) Act 1993 to equalising access to these rights for *all* employees after two years of service.

One area where the community clearly thinks differences in employment rights are not appropriate is in the area of maternity benefits. The Directive on maternity provisions which has now been approved will mean that from October 1994 *all* women, regardless of length of service or hours worked, will be entitled to 14 weeks maternity leave and to not be dismissed for reasons of pregnancy. There are also requirements to protect pregnant and nursing women from hazards at work. This may mean adjustment of duties or, where this is not possible, leave for the period of the confinement or nursing period. The Directive does not reduce any existing superior provision. The major impact of this Directive in the colleges will be in relation to the employment of part-time staff.

The Working Time Directive will have limited impact as it is mostly concerned with night work and rest days. However, the introduction of a statutory right to paid holiday will again have implications for the terms and conditions of our part-time work force.

The Directive concerned with the distortion of competition is still being debated as several member states are unhappy with some of the provisions. The article which will have most significance for colleges will be that which restricts the use of fixed-term contracts. There is no indication at present when this Directive will be agreed.

The need for brevity in this chapter precludes further comment on other Directives but from the brief outlines above the impact of legislation on working practices, employment policies and budgets can be seen to be significant for colleges.

The sheer scale of legislative change in the 1990s will force it on to the agendas of human resource managers. If it does not force itself on to the agenda of the strategic planners in colleges then there is the potential for considerable chaos when changes of direction have to be implemented owing to legal requirements; changes which could be costly to implement in organisational, financial and human terms.

Conclusions

Many external influences are predictable, some are not. Let us at least plan for the predictable.

The mid and late 1990s present an enormous opportunity for change in the ways we manage and develop our staff in colleges. External forces can be seen as opportunities or impediments. I hope they are seen as opportunities.

To end as begun with a quotation:

> The events of the 90s will create such demands for change upon organisations that many will go under. And the major reason they will do so is that they will fail to recruit and retain the people they need to help them change. People make the place, and people set the pace.
> Professor Peter Herriot

References

Equal Pay Directive (1975) 75/117/EEC

Equal Treatment Directive (1976) 76/207/EEC

Foster and ors. v British Gas plc (1990) European Court of Justice 12.7.90 (Source: Incomes Data Services. **Employment law cases. Race and sex discrimination, equal pay volume 2)**

Francovich and ors. v Italian Republic (1991) European Court of Jsutce 19.11.91 (Source: Incomes Data Services. **Employment law cases. Race and sex discrimination, equal pay volume 2)**

Herriot, Professor Peter (1989) **Recruitment in the '90s.** IPM

Index

external agencies
  influences on college planning 35, 99
  influence on staff training 37
  strategic alliances 14
  see also Europe

F

financial cuts 13

financial management 25, 55

five-year plans 13

flexibility, in human resources
  management 50-1

free movement, within Europe 103

further education, narrow views of 49-50

Further Education Funding Council 11,
  50, 76

Further Education Staff College 33

Further Education Unit 38

Further & Higher Education Act 1992 55

G

generic assessor training 38

governing bodies
  appraisal of principal 75
  powers 48
  remuneration committee 75
  role in appraisal process 76-7
  staff recruitment 61-2

Grant-Related In-Service Training 34

Grants for Education Support &
  Training 34

Guidance & Counselling Lead Body 38

Guildford College of Further and Higher
  Education 25

H

human resources development
  change 47, 51-9
  co-ordination of college organisational
    cycles 44-6

human resources management 9, 55
  flexibility 51

human resources planning 61-2

I

incentive schemes 57

incorporation
  pressures for change 49
  specialist staff appointments 92
  tensions of role changes 54
  transition period 13, 20

induction 16
  new staff 67

industrial relations, in further education
  76

information technology, in-house training
  programmes 42

Inner London Education Authority 13

INSET 35-7

in-service training initiatives 34

inspection, HMI rejection of appraisal 85
  see also audit

interview procedure 66

institutional mapping 28

Investors in People 11-14, 78
  standard 15
  standard attainment 15-16

IS 09000 26

iterative planning processes 16

student support services 26, 92-3

success factors 24, 25

support, for new staff 16

support staff
administrative 53
changing roles 91-3
impact of incorporation 13
involvement in team meetings 82
recruitment and selection 62, 63
specialisation 54

T

targets, national 11

teaching, deprofessionalisation 98

teaching teams concept 92-3, 98

team meetings 82

terms and conditions of service 18, 48, 49
changing 50-2
see also contracts

total quality 22, 24, 26
action model 23
development activities 27

total quality management 21-2
benefits 27

trade unions 55, 76, 95
concerns over appraisal 72
legal challenges 103
see also NATFHE

training
eligibility 36
entitlement 36
external provision 18
in-house 37, 42-4
interviewers 62
re-training packages 64, 65

Training and Development Lead Body 38

training and education targets 11

training and enterprise councils 11, 14

training objectives, and staff development 15

training policy statements 40-1

U

unit of resource, and efficiency 50

UNISON 76

V

validity, of course programmes 30

values 27, 82
reward system 91

W

women 18
employment directives 106
principles 82

work, concepts of 95